**Editor**
Eric Migliaccio

**Managing Editor**
Ina Massler Levin, M.A.

**Editor-in-Chief**
Sharon Coan, M.S. Ed.

**Illustrator**
Ken Tunell

**Cover Artist**
Barb Lorseyedi

**Art Manager**
Kevin Barnes

**Art Director**
CJac Froshay

**Imaging**
Rosa C. See

**Product Manager**
Phil Garcia

**Publisher**
Mary D. Smith, M.S. Ed.

# Mastering Vocabulary

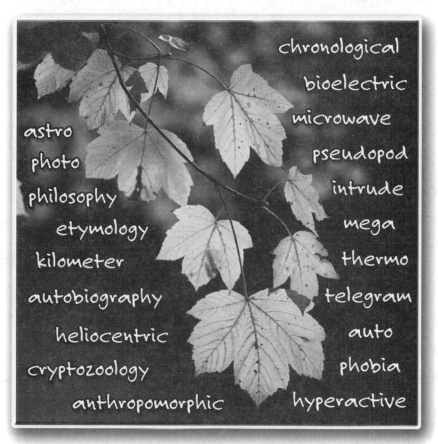

**Author**

*Stephanie Riddle, M.A. Ed.*

Teacher
Created
Resources

***Teacher Created Resources, Inc.***
6421 Industry Way
Westminster, CA 92683
www.teachercreated.com
**ISBN: 978-0-7439-3433-6**
*©2004 Teacher Created Resources, Inc.*
Reprinted, 2010
Made in U.S.A.

# Table of Contents

# Table of Contents *(cont.)*

# Introduction

In her book *Words: English Roots and How They Grow*, Margaret Ernst likened the science and study of etymology to trees. Just like a botanist learns a lot from studying parts of trees, an etymologist learns much from studying parts of words.

This book is designed as an introduction to etymology. Each weekly exercise introduces students to approximately ten Greek and Latin roots. They use these roots in a matching section, where ten words containing a root from the list go with definitions. Next, students write out definitions to five words, each word containing a root from the list. Finally, in the last section, students work with suffixes, which determine a word's part of speech.

The word parts used in this workbook will enable students to improve Standardized Aptitude Test scores, increase their existing vocabulary, and improve reading and comprehension. The teaching recommendations that follow the introduction suggest ways of further incorporating etymology into the middle-school classroom.

## How to Use this Book

1. Introduce students to etymology and assign the first weekly unit.

2. Grade and discuss the assignment.

3. Quiz students at the end of the week.

4. Since each lesson builds on the previous assignments, encourage students to keep all worksheets. The lessons are designed to review completed work, as well as introduce new material.

5. After each group of four units, there is a cumulative review. It includes most or all of the learned word parts, though the parts are found in different words. Most words should be found in the *American Heritage Dictionary*. Students simply match each word with its appropriate definition.

6. Some lessons were designed with literature curriculum in mind. For instance, units 21–24 should be used in conjunction with mythology. These units have no individual quizzes but a cumulative one at the end.

7. Units 13–16 were designed to address different skills. Unit 13, for example, focuses primarily on using affixes. It enables students to put together words of their own. Units 14 and 15 focus on two of the most well-known word parts: *phobia* and *logy*. Unit 16 centers on word trees.

8. Units 29–32 are cumulative reviews of the word parts and concepts taught over the course of the year.

# Introduction *(cont.)*

## Teaching Suggestions

The study of etymology can be effective *and* entertaining. The suggestions that follow will enable you to make learning the building blocks of our language fun.

- When beginning etymology, point out the zaniness of the language. "Why is *phonetic* not spelled phonetically? Why is it so hard to remember how to spell *mnemonic*? Why is the word *abbreviation* so long?" (Lederer, *Crazy English*, 5) Richard Lederer's book contains more gems to share in class. They are all valid questions, and the students will enjoy trying to answer them.

- The idea of etymology is new to most students. When explaining the definitions of roots, affixes (prefixes and suffixes), derivatives, etc., present them with the following word:

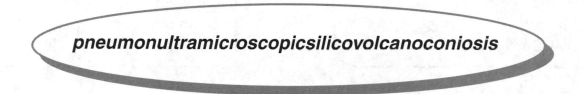

**pneumonultramicroscopicsilicovolcanoconiosis**

Begin by asking if anyone would like to tackle the pronunciation of this word. Then ask students what parts of the word look familiar. From that point on, put all the parts together in a logical definition. The students will find that their definition is similar to the actual meaning. That exercise engages them in a fun but meaningful introduction to etymology. (***Note:*** *pneumonultramicroscopicsilicovolcanoconiosis* is a medical condition known as "black lung disease.")

- In *The Teaching of High School English*, J.N. Hook and William H. Evans offer several suggestions for teaching etymology. One idea is called "One Word Led to Another." "Starting with the word *kilometer*, the vocational students thought of two other words based on either *kilo* or *meter*, then two words based on each of the new words, and so on. They thus learned much about root words and families of words" (299). Using this activity with dictionaries makes a good exercise. (See page 6 for "Word Tree Worksheet.")

- Halloween is a good time to discuss all the strange and unusual phobias that exist, and it's an excellent way of reviewing or learning more roots. In Charles Harrington Elster's *There's a Word for It!*, chapter six claims to be "the world's greatest gathering of phobias" (1996, 135). He includes 600 words for these common and sometimes bizarre fears. Richard Lederer's *Crazy English* contains a chapter on phobias, and his book *The Play of Words: Fun and Games for Language Lovers* supplies a phobia quiz. Aside from testing their knowledge on the quiz, these phobias allow students to be creative with bulletin boards or scary stories.

# Word Tree Worksheet

**Directions:** Beginning with one word, create a word tree. Your first and second words must contain some part of the first word. Beneath the two new words, give their definitions. Then use parts from Words 2 and 3 to create Words 4, 5, and 6, and define those words, as well. Here is an example:

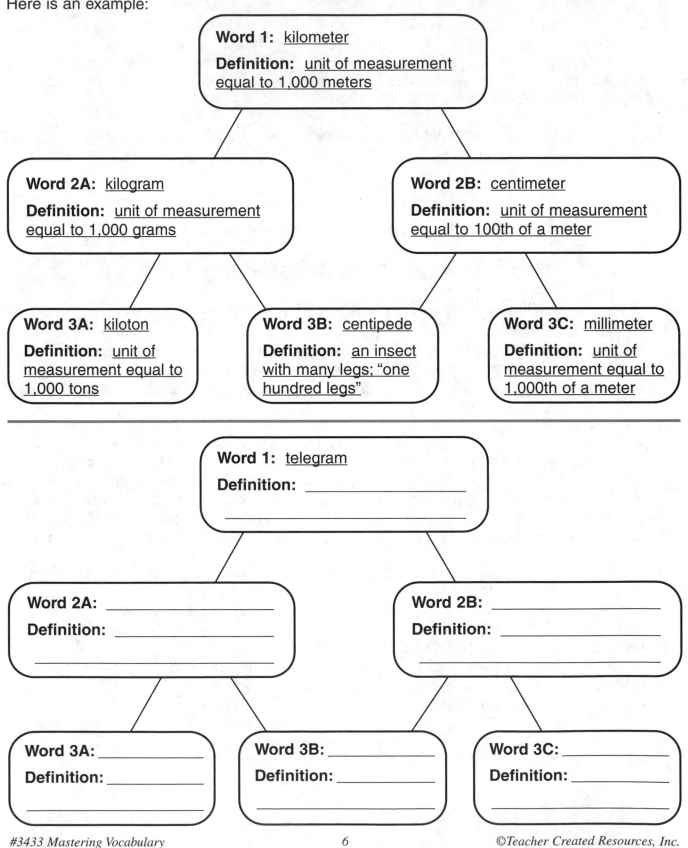

**Word 1:** kilometer

**Definition:** unit of measurement equal to 1,000 meters

**Word 2A:** kilogram

**Definition:** unit of measurement equal to 1,000 grams

**Word 2B:** centimeter

**Definition:** unit of measurement equal to 100th of a meter

**Word 3A:** kiloton

**Definition:** unit of measurement equal to 1,000 tons

**Word 3B:** centipede

**Definition:** an insect with many legs; "one hundred legs"

**Word 3C:** millimeter

**Definition:** unit of measurement equal to 1,000th of a meter

**Word 1:** telegram

**Definition:** _____

**Word 2A:** _____

**Definition:** _____

**Word 2B:** _____

**Definition:** _____

**Word 3A:** _____

**Definition:** _____

**Word 3B:** _____

**Definition:** _____

**Word 3C:** _____

**Definition:** _____

# References

What follows is a list of books you may find useful in addition to this workbook.

Costello, R. (editor). *The American Heritage College Dictionary: Third Edition.* Houghton Mifflin Company, 1993.

Elster, C. Harrington. *There's a Word For It!* Pocket Books, 1996.

Ernst, Margaret. *English Roots and How They Grow.* Alfred A. Knopf, 1966.

Hook, J.N. and William H. Evans. *The Teaching of High School English.* Macmillan Publishing Company, 1982.

Lederer, Richard. *Crazy English: The Ultimate Joy Ride Through Our Language.* Pocket Books, 1998.

————. *The Play of Words: Fun and Games for Language Lovers.* Pocket Books, 1991.

Morse-Cluley, E. and R. Read. *Webster's New World Power Vocabulary.* Macmillan Publishing Company, 1994.

Romine, J. and H. Ehrlich. *Quick Vocabulary Power: A Self-Teaching Guide.* John Wiley & Sons, 1996.

# Vocabulary List

| Word Part | Meaning |
| --- | --- |
| anthrop(o) | man |
| anti, ant | against |
| arch | first, chief, ancient, ruler |
| astro | star |
| auto | self |
| bene | good, well |
| bio | life |
| centri | center |
| chrono | time |
| cide | (to) kill |
| crac | rule |
| crypto | hidden, secret |
| dem(o) | people |
| gam(os) | marriage |
| gen | birth, race, kind |
| geo | Earth |
| gram | something written |
| graph(y) | to write |
| helio | sun |
| hydr | water |

# Vocabulary List *(cont.)*

| Word Part | Meaning |
|---|---|
| hyper | over, excessive |
| hypo | under, less than |
| logy | science, study of |
| mega | great, large |
| meter | a device for measuring |
| micro | small |
| mis | hate, bad, wrong |
| moro | fool |
| nom | knowledge, rule |
| nomen, nomin, nym | name |
| path | feelings, sufferings, disease |
| peri | around, near |
| philo | love of |
| phobia | fear of |
| phon | sound |
| photo | light |
| pod, ped | foot |
| polis, polit | city, citizen |
| poly | many |
| pseudo | false |
| pyr | fire |
| scop | to see |
| soph | wisdom |
| syn, sym | same, together with |
| tele | far |
| thermo | heat |

# Unit 1 Words

| Word Part | Meaning |
|---|---|
| auto- | self |
| bio- | life |
| centri- | center |
| chrono- | time |
| crypto- | hidden, secret |
| geo- | Earth |
| -gram | something written |
| -graphy | to write |

| Word Part | Meaning |
|---|---|
| helio- | the sun |
| -logy | science of |
| -meter | a device for measuring |
| moro- | fool |
| philo- | love of |
| -phobia | fear, hatred |
| soph- | wisdom |

## Matching

_____ 1. autobiography

_____ 2. autograph

_____ 3. biology

_____ 4. chronometer

_____ 5. cryptogram

_____ 6. geology

_____ 7. heliocentric

_____ 8. moron

_____ 9. philosophy

_____ 10. phobophobia

A. one's own signature

B. the fear of fear itself

C. a foolish person

D. the love of wisdom

E. a clock that keeps accurate time

F. the study of Earth

G. something written in secret code

H. the sun as the center

I. the study of life

J. a book written about the author by the author

## Definitions

**Directions:** Define the words below. The words in italics are fabricated.

1. sophomore _____

_____

2. *biophobia* _____

_____

3. *autocryptology* _____

_____

4. *chronophile* _____

_____

5. geometry _____

_____

# Unit 1 Words *(cont.)*

## Affix Practice

**Directions:** Fill in the blanks as directed. A sample for the word *intrude* has been given. List only one verb, adjective, etc. You may not find one of each.

**Word:** _____ intrude _____

**Root Element:** _____ trud _____     **Meaning:** _____ to thrust _____

**Affix Element:** _____ in _____     **Meaning:** _____ in, into _____

| Verb | Adjective | Adverb | Noun |
|------|-----------|--------|------|
| intrude | intrusive | intrusively | intruder,  intrusion |

**Word:** _____ geology _____

**Root Element:** _____ logy _____     **Meaning:** _____ study of _____

**Affix Element:** _____     **Meaning:** _____

| Verb | Adjective | Adverb | Noun |
|------|-----------|--------|------|
|  |  |  |  |

## Extended Activity

**Directions:** Make up and briefly define five words using the roots above or other roots.

| Word | Definition |
|------|------------|
| 1. |  |
| 2. |  |
| 3. |  |
| 4. |  |
| 5. |  |

# Unit 1 Quiz

## Word Roots

**Directions:** Identify the root and write it on the first line. On the next, tell what the root means. (Numbers 3, 6, and 9 have two roots in the word. Name and define them both.) Then define the whole word on the last line.

1. **zoology**
   Root: _____
   Root Meaning: _____
   Word Definition: _____

2. **millimeter**
   Root: _____
   Root Meaning: _____
   Word Definition: _____

3. **chronological**
   Roots: _____
   Root Meanings: _____
   Word Definition: _____

4. **arachnophobia**
   Root: _____
   Root Meaning: _____
   Word Definition: _____

5. **telegram**
   Root: _____
   Root Meaning: _____
   Word Definition: _____

6. **sophomore**
   Roots: _____
   Root Meanings: _____
   Word Definition: _____

7. **Helios**
   Root: _____
   Root Meaning: _____
   Word Definition: _____

8. **benephile**
   Root: _____
   Root Meaning: _____
   Word Definition: _____

9. **biography**
   Roots: _____
   Root Meanings: _____
   Word Definition: _____

## Matching

**Directions:** Match each word to its definition.

_____ 10. cryptology

_____ 11. bibliophile

_____ 12. automotive

_____ 13. centrist

_____ 14. sophisticated

_____ 15. heliotrope

_____ 16. bioelectric

_____ 17. entomology

_____ 18. audiophile

_____ 19. pathology

_____ 20. chronometer

A. moving by itself; self-propelled

B. knowledgeable in the ways of the world

C. study of secret messages

D. electric current generated by living tissue

E. one in the political center

F. the study of insects

G. any of various plants that turn to the sun

H. one who loves books

I. one who loves music

J. a device for measuring time

K. the science or study of disease

# Unit 2

| Word Part | Meaning |
|---|---|
| anthrop(o)- | man |
| mis- | hate, bad, wrong |
| arch- | first, chief, ancient, ruler of government |
| -crac | rule |
| -cide | (to) kill |
| gen- | birth, race, kind |

| Word Part | Meaning |
|---|---|
| thermo- | heat |
| tele- | far |
| poly- | many |
| dem(o)- | people |
| nomen, nomin, nym- | name |
| -gam(os) | marriage |

## Matching

_____ 1. archeology (archaeology)

_____ 2. democracy

_____ 3. genocide

_____ 4. misogamy

_____ 5. nominate

_____ 6. philanthropy

_____ 7. polygamy

_____ 8. telegram

_____ 9. thermometer

_____ 10. thermophobia

A. love for mankind

B. study of ancient civilizations

C. government for the people by the people

D. union of many spouses

E. killing of a racial group

F. written communication that is sent

G. hatred of marriage

H. instrument that measures heat

I. to name or appoint

J. fear of heat

## Definitions

**Directions:** Define the words below. The words in italics are fabricated.

1. *autogamy* _____

_____

2. telemeter _____

_____

3. *biocide* _____

_____

4. graphology _____

_____

5. cryptonym _____

# Unit 2

## Affix Practice

Fill in the blanks as directed.  A sample for the word *intrude* has been given.  List only one verb, adjective, etc. You may not find one of each.

**Word:** _____ intrud _____

**Root Element:** _____ trud _____     **Meaning:** _____ to thrust _____

**Affix Element:** _____ in _____     **Meaning:** _____ in, into _____

| Verb | Adjective | Adverb | Noun |
|------|-----------|--------|------|
| intrude | intrusive | intrusively | intruder,  intrusion |

**Word:** _____ synonym _____

**Root Element:** _____ (o)nym _____     **Meaning:** _____ name _____

**Affix Element:** _____     **Meaning:** _____

| Verb | Adjective | Adverb | Noun |
|------|-----------|--------|------|
|      |           |        |      |

## Extended Activity

**Extra Word:** archaic

**Definition:** that which has ceased to be used except for special purposes, as in poetry or church ritual.  Some words like *thou* are archaic.

**Directions:** List as many words as you can think of that would be considered archaic.

_____      _____

_____      _____

_____      _____

_____      _____

# Unit 2 Quiz

## Word Roots

**Directions:** Identify the root and write it on the first line. On the next, tell what the root means. Then define the whole word on the last line.

1. **bigamy**
   Root: _____
   Root Meaning: _____
   Word Definition: _____

2. **nominate**
   Root: _____
   Root Meaning: _____
   Word Definition: _____

3. **eponym**
   Root: _____
   Root Meaning: _____
   Word Definition: _____

4. **telephoto lens**
   Root: _____
   Root Meaning: _____
   Word Definition: _____

5. **matricide**
   Root: _____
   Root Meaning: _____
   Word Definition: _____

6. **polygon**
   Root: _____
   Root Meaning _____
   Word Definition: _____

7. **monarchy**
   Root: _____
   Root Meaning: _____
   Word Definition: _____

8. **misguided**
   Root: _____
   Root Meaning: _____
   Word Definition: _____

9. **gene**
   Root: _____
   Root Meaning: _____
   Word Definition: _____

10. **epidemic**
   Root: _____
   Root Meaning: _____
   Word Definition: _____

# Unit 2 Quiz *(cont.)*

## Matching

**Directions:** Match the following words to their definitions.

_____ 11. monogamy

_____ 12. demography

_____ 13. archeologist

_____ 14. generate

_____ 15. polynomial

_____ 16. anthropologist

_____ 17. aristocracy

_____ 18. telephony

_____ 19. misapply

_____ 20. pesticide

A. a person trained to excavate ruins and reconstruct the life of ancient civilizations

B. gives birth to excitement

C. a person who studies man(kind)

D. the science of recording people

E. rule by the highest social class

F. to apply wrongly

G. act of having one marriage

H. a chemical used to kill pests

I. transmission of sound through distant points

J. consisting of more than two names or terms

# Unit 3

| Word Part | Meaning |
|---|---|
| phon- | sound |
| photo- | light |
| bene- | good, well |
| hydr- | water |
| pseudo- | false |
| astro- | star |

| Word Part | Meaning |
|---|---|
| mega- | great, large |
| micro- | small |
| nom- | knowledge, rule |
| path- | feelings, sufferings, disease |

## Matching

_____ 1. astrology

_____ 2. astronomy

_____ 3. benephile

_____ 4. hydrant

_____ 5. megaphone

_____ 6. micrometer

_____ 7. pathology

_____ 8. phonograph

_____ 9. pseudonym

_____ 10. telephone

A. a machine reproducing sound

B. far reaching sound

C. good person

D. large outlet for water

E. study of stars

F. instrument used to increase loudness of voice

G. measures very small things

H. systemized knowledge of stars

I. false name

J. study of diseases

## Definitions

**Directions:** Define the words below. The word in italics is fabricated.

1. autonomy _____

_____

2. hydrometer _____

_____

3. photograph _____

_____

4. *megastrophobia* _____

_____

5. microbiology _____

_____

## Affix Practice

**Directions:** Fill in the blanks as directed. A sample has been given. List only one verb, adjective, etc. You may not find one of each.

**Word:** _____intrude_____

**Root Element:** _____trud_____     **Meaning:** _____to thrust_____

**Affix Element:** _____in_____     **Meaning:** _____in, into_____

| Verb | Adjective | Adverb | Noun |
|------|-----------|--------|------|
| intrude | intrusive | intrusively | intruder, intrusion |

**Word:** _____beneficial_____

**Root Element:** _____fic_____     **Meaning:** _____to make do_____

**Affix Element:** _____     **Meaning:** _____

| Verb | Adjective | Adverb | Noun |
|------|-----------|--------|------|
|  |  |  |  |

## Extended Activity

**Extra Word:** pseudonym

**Definition:** an assumed name; "false name"

**Directions:** Many authors use pseudonyms instead of their real names when they publish their books. Can you name any authors who do this? Below are the names of a few authors who use pseudonyms. Do research to find their real names. Also, name one famous book that the author wrote.

| Pseudonym | Actual Name | Famous Book |
|-----------|-------------|-------------|
| Dr. Seuss |  |  |
| Mark Twain |  |  |
| George Orwell |  |  |
| O. Henry |  |  |

# Unit 3 Quiz

## Word Roots

**Directions:** Identify the root and write it on the first line.  On the next, tell what the root means.  Then define the whole word on the last line.

1. **microscope**
   Root: _____
   Root Meaning: _____
   Word Definition: _____

2. **pseudopod**
   Root: _____
   Root Meaning: _____
   Word Definition: _____

3. **hydroplane**
   Root: _____
   Root Meaning: _____
   Word Definition: _____

4. **agronomy**
   Root: _____
   Root Meaning: _____
   Word Definition: _____

5. **benefactor**
   Root: _____
   Root Meaning: _____
   Word Definition: _____

6. **megalith**
   Root: _____
   Root Meaning: _____
   Word Definition: _____

7. **astronautics**
   Root: _____
   Root Meaning: _____
   Word Definition: _____

8. **pathos**
   Root: _____
   Root Meaning: _____
   Word Definition: _____

9. **photocopy**
   Root: _____
   Root Meaning: _____
   Word Definition: _____

10. **phonetic**
    Root: _____
    Root Meaning: _____
    Word Definition: _____

# Unit 3 Quiz *(cont.)*

## Matching

**Directions:** Match the words to their definitions.

_____ 11. sympathy

_____ 12. metronome

_____ 13. photosynthesis

_____ 14. polyphonic

_____ 15. megalopolis

_____ 16. microcosm

_____ 17. hydroponics

_____ 18. benefit

_____ 19. astrophysics

_____ 20. pseudonym

A. music that has many voices or sounds

B. greatest concentration of population identified by large city

C. the science of growing plants in water

D. sharing someone else's suffering

E. an advantage; to be helpful

F. science that studies the physical and chemical nature of stars

G. a clock that "rules the measure"

H. small universe

I. pen name, false name

J. plants use the energy of light to synthesize carbohydrates from carbon dioxide and water

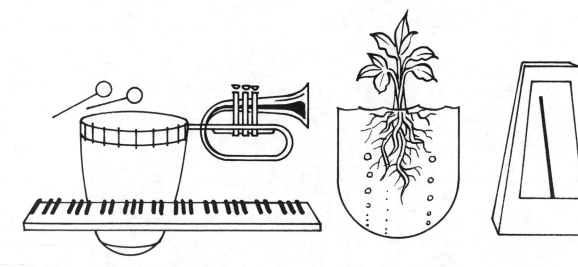

# Unit 4

| Word Part | Meaning | Word Part | Meaning |
|---|---|---|---|
| -pod, ped- | foot | syn-, sym- | same, together with |
| -scop- | to see | pyr- | fire |
| hyper- | over, excessive | hypo- | under, less than |
| anti-, ant- | against | -polis, polit- | city, citizen |
| peri- | around, near | | |

## Matching

_____ 1. antibiotic

_____ 2. hyperthermia

_____ 3. hypothermia

_____ 4. Indianapolis

_____ 5. perimeter

_____ 6. pyrography

_____ 7. sympathy

_____ 8. synchronize

_____ 9. telescope

_____ 10. tripod

A. measurement around something

B. instrument used to see far away

C. burning designs on wood

D. above-normal body temperature

E. to do together at the same time

F. city of Indiana

G. a three-footed stand to hold a camera

H. below-normal body temperature

I. a medicine that fights living bacteria

J. sharing someone else's feelings or sufferings

## Definitions

**Directions:** Define the words below.

1. cosmopolitan _____

_____

2. antipathy _____

_____

3. periscope _____

_____

4. megalopolis _____

_____

5. pyrophobia _____

_____

# Unit 4 *(cont.)*

## Affix Practice

**Directions:** Fill in the blanks as directed.  A sample has been given.  List only one verb, adjective, etc. You may not find one of each.

**Word:** _____ intrude _____

**Root Element:** _____ trud _____     **Meaning:** _____ to thrust _____

**Affix Element:** _____ in _____     **Meaning:** _____ in, into _____

| Verb | Adjective | Adverb | Noun |
|------|-----------|--------|------|
| intrude | intrusive | intrusively | intruder,  intrusion |

**Word:** _____ politics _____

**Root Element:** _____ polit _____     **Meaning:** _____ city, citizen _____

**Affix Element:** _____ none _____     **Meaning:** _____ none _____

| Verb | Adjective | Adverb | Noun |
|------|-----------|--------|------|
|  |  |  |  |

## Extended Activity

**Extra Word:** hyperbole

**Definition:** exaggeration for effect, not meant to be taken literally

**Directions:** List three examples of hyperbole.  (Think of exaggerations you might make.)

1. _____

2. _____

3. _____

# Unit 4 Quiz

## Word Roots

**Directions:** Identify the root and write it on the first line.  On the next, tell what the root means.  Then define the whole word on the last line.

1. **politics**
   Root: _____
   Root Meaning: _____
   Word Definition: _____

2. **antitrust**
   Root: _____
   Root Meaning: _____
   Word Definition: _____

3. **horoscope**
   Root: _____
   Root Meaning: _____
   Word Definition: _____

4. **pyromaniac**
   Root: _____
   Root Meaning: _____
   Word Definition: _____

5. **podiatrist**
   Root: _____
   Root Meaning: _____
   Word Definition: _____

6. **hypodermic**
   Root: _____
   Root Meaning: _____
   Word Definition: _____

7. **hypercritical**
   Root: _____
   Root Meaning: _____
   Word Definition: _____

8. **pericardium**
   Root: _____
   Root Meaning: _____
   Word Definition: _____

9. **symposium**
   Root: _____
   Root Meaning: _____
   Word Definition: _____

10. **pedicure**
    Root: _____
    Root Meaning: _____
    Word Definition: _____

## Matching

**Directions:** Match the words to their definitions.

_____ 11. pedestrian

_____ 12. metropolis

_____ 13. antisocial

_____ 14. stethoscope

_____ 15. pyrotechnics

_____ 16. hypoglycemia

_____ 17. hyperbole

_____ 18. perigee

_____ 19. synonym

_____ 20. politician

A. a condition of the moon being near the sun

B. contrary or harmful to the existing social order

C. one who walks

D. a citizen who takes active part in government

E. an instrument used "to see" the chest

F. the making or display of fireworks

G. overstatement, exaggeration

H. words that mean approximately the same thing

I. large city; large urban center

J. an abnormally low level of glucose in the blood

# Units 1–4 Review

**Directions:** Match the definitions on page 27 to the words below.

_____ 1. antibiotic

_____ 2. aristocracy

_____ 3. astrophobia

_____ 4. autocrat

_____ 5. autonomous

_____ 6. benefit

_____ 7. chronology

_____ 8. cosmopolite

_____ 9. cryptology

_____ 10. demography

_____ 11. geocentric

_____ 12. Heliopolis

_____ 13. herbicide

_____ 14. hydrophobia

_____ 15. hyperthermia

_____ 16. hypothermia

_____ 17. megalopolis

_____ 18. microphone

_____ 19. misanthrope

_____ 20. misnomer

_____ 21. monarch

_____ 22. monogamous

_____ 23. moronic

_____ 24. pathetic

_____ 25. pedal

_____ 26. philosopher

_____ 27. photophobia

_____ 28. polygraph

_____ 29. pseudopod

_____ 30. psychogenic

_____ 31. pyre

_____ 32. sophisticated

_____ 33. synonym

_____ 34. telegram

_____ 35. telescope

_____ 36. thermometer

# Units 1–4 Review (cont.)

## Definitions

A. fear of stars

B. a person who hates mankind

C. chief ruler

D. a study of time sequence

E. the science of recording people

F. based on one marriage at a time

G. having its origin (birth) in the mind

H. fear of water

I. study of secret messages

J. small sound

K. greatest concentration of citizens

L. a wrong name

M. relating to self-rule

N. words that mean the same thing

O. marked by suffering

P. lover of wisdom

Q. a foot-operated lever

R. world citizen

S. "many records"

T. fire used to cremate corpses

U. an instrument to see far away

V. a medicine that fights living bacteria

W. Earth as the center of the universe

X. rule of highest social class

Y. instrument that measures heat

Z. false foot

AA. city of worship for sun god

BB. a substance used to kill plants (weeds)

CC. something that enhances well-being

DD. fear of light

EE. above-normal body temperature

FF. below-normal body temperature

GG. foolish

HH. "ruler of oneself"

II. written communication that is sent

JJ. wise in the ways of the world

# Units 1–4 Quiz

## Matching, Part I

**Directions:** Match each word to its definition.

_____ 1. cryptology                    _____ 6. pyre

_____ 2. misanthrope                 _____ 7. misnomer

_____ 3. hydrophobia                 _____ 8. astrophobia

_____ 4. psychogenic                 _____ 9. pseudopod

_____ 5. benefit                          _____ 10. moronic

A. fear of stars                             F. study of secret messages

B. "false foot"                               G. fear of water

C. error in calling someone's name    H. having its origin (birth) in the mind

D. foolish                                      I. fire used to cremate corpses

E. something that enhances well-being   J. a person who hates mankind

## Matching, Part II

**Directions:** Match each word to its definition.

_____ 11. demography               _____ 16. photophobia

_____ 12. megalopolis               _____ 17. pathetic

_____ 13. monarch                    _____ 18. synonym

_____ 14. antibiotic                   _____ 19. thermometer

_____ 15. autocrat                     _____ 20. cosmopolite

A. world citizen                            F. the science of recording people

B. a medicine that fights living bacteria   G. "ruler of oneself"

C. marked by suffering                  H. chief ruler

D. words that mean the same thing   I. greatest concentration of citizens

E. instrument that measures heat    J. fear of light

# Units 1–4 Quiz *(cont.)*

## Matching, Part III

**Directions:** Match each word to its definition.

_____ 21. chronology

_____ 22. herbicide

_____ 23. autonomous

_____ 24. hypothermia

_____ 25. monogamous

_____ 26. pedal

_____ 27. aristocracy

_____ 28. hyperthermia

_____ 29. telegram

_____ 30. philosopher

_____ 31. microphone

_____ 32. polygraph

_____ 33. Heliopolis

_____ 34. telescope

_____ 35. geocentric

---

A. a substance used to kill plants (weeds)

B. above normal body temperature

C. city of worship for sun god

D. lover of wisdom

E. an instrument to see far away

F. a foot-operated lever

G. a study of time sequence

H. Earth as the center of universe

I. relating to self-rule

J. "small sound"

K. below normal body temperature

L. rule of highest social class

M. based on one marriage at a time

N. written communication that is sent

O. "many records"

# Vocabulary List

| Word Part | Meaning |
| --- | --- |
| amor | love |
| aqu(a) | water |
| bi, di, du | two |
| capit | head |
| card | heart |
| carn | flesh |
| cent | hundred |
| circum | around |
| corp | body |
| dec | ten |
| demi | half |
| dict | to say, speak |
| duc(t) | lead |
| enne | nine |
| equi | equal |
| frater | brother |
| gyn | woman |
| hemi | half |
| hept | seven |
| hex | six |
| kilo | thousand |
| mal | bad |
| mat(er) | mother |
| mill | thousand |

# Vocabulary List *(cont.)*

| Word Part | Meaning |
|---|---|
| mon, mono | one |
| multi | many |
| non, nov(em) | nine |
| oct | eight |
| omni | all |
| pat(er) | father |
| ped | child |
| penta | five |
| quad(u) | four |
| quart | fourth |
| quin | five |
| scribe, script | write |
| semi | half |
| sept | seven |
| sex(t) | six |
| sol | alone |
| soror | sister |
| spec, spic | look, see |
| tetr(o) | four |
| the | god |
| tri | three |
| uni | one |
| val | farewell |
| vir | man |

# Unit 5

| Latin | Meaning | Greek |
|---|---|---|
| uni | one | mon, mono |
| bi, du | two | di |
| tri | three | tri |
| quad(ru), quart | four, fourth | tetr(o) |
| quin | five | penta |
| sex(t) | six | hex |
| sept | seven | hept |
| oct | eight | oct |
| non, nov(em) | nine | enne |
| dec | ten | dec |

## Matching

_____ 1. biannual

_____ 2. decimeter

_____ 3. duet

_____ 4. monogram

_____ 5. November

_____ 6. pentagon

_____ 7. quarter

_____ 8. quintuplet(s)

_____ 9. trilogy

_____ 10. unique

A. a design composed on one initial

B. happening twice a year

C. one-tenth of a meter

D. a group of five offspring born in a single birth

E. a group of two (musicians)

F. a study of three dramatic or literary works

G. 9th month (of original Roman calendar)

H. one-fourth of a dollar

I. a five-sided figure

J. only one of its kind; extraordinary

# Unit 5

## Definitions

**Directions:** Define the real words below. Use a dictionary, if necessary.

1. septennial _____

_____

2. triumvirate _____

_____

3. decade _____

_____

4. sextet _____

_____

5. unicorn _____

_____

6. nonagon _____

_____

7. October _____

_____

8. duplicate _____

_____

9. bigamy _____

_____

10. tripod _____

_____

## Extended Activity

**Extra Words:** anno domini

**Definition:** These are the two words that make up the abbreviation "A.D.," as in 1000 A.D. Literally, the words mean "in the year of the Lord." They refer to all the years since the birth of Jesus Christ.

**Directions:** Answer this question: Why is this century referred to as the 21st century even though, numerically, the year is in the 2000s?

_____

_____

# Unit 5 Quiz

**Word Roots**

**Directions:** Identify the root and write it on the first line. On the next, tell what the root means. Then define the whole word on the last line.

1. **September**
   Root: _____
   Root Meaning: _____
   Word Definition: _____

2. **pentadactyl**
   Root: _____
   Root Meaning: _____
   Word Definition: _____

3. **unicycle**
   Root: _____
   Root Meaning: _____
   Word Definition: _____

4. **triad**
   Root: _____
   Root Meaning: _____
   Word Definition: _____

5. **quadruplets**
   Root: _____
   Root Meaning: _____
   Word Definition: _____

6. **binoculars**
   Root: _____
   Root Meaning: _____
   Word Definition: _____

7. **hexagon**
   Root: _____
   Root Meaning: _____
   Word Definition: _____

8. **decathlon**
   Root: _____
   Root Meaning: _____
   Word Definition: _____

9. **quintuplets**
   Root: _____
   Root Meaning: _____
   Word Definition: _____

10. **duel**
    Root: _____
    Root Meaning: _____
    Word Definition: _____

# Unit 5 Quiz *(cont.)*

## Matching

**Directions:** Match each word to its definition.

_____ 11. bifurcate

_____ 12. pentathlon

_____ 13. nonagon

_____ 14. unilateral

_____ 15. quadrangle

_____ 16. bicentennial

_____ 17. sextuplets

_____ 18. octogenarian

_____ 19. decimal

_____ 20. tripartite

A. of, relating to, involving, or affecting only one side

B. six babies born at a single birth

C. to divide into two branches or parts

D. a period of two hundred years

E. a person between the ages of 80 and 89

F. based on the number 10

G. a nine-sided figure

H. a rectangular area bordered on all four sides by buildings

I. divided into three parts

J. an athletic contest consisting of five events

# Unit 6

| Word Part | Meaning | Word Part | Meaning |
|-----------|---------|-----------|---------|
| multi- | many | equi- | equal |
| semi- | half | hemi- | half |
| demi- | half | omni- | all |
| sol- | alone | cent- | hundred |
| mill- | thousand | kilo- | thousand |

## Matching

_____ 1. century

_____ 2. demigod

_____ 3. equinox

_____ 4. hemihydrate

_____ 5. kilogram

_____ 6. millipede

_____ 7. multiply

_____ 8. omniscient

_____ 9. semicircle

_____ 10. solitary

A. to increase the amount; to grow in number

B. either of two times in the year when day and night are equal in length

C. half a circle

D. having total knowledge; knowing everything

E. a male being, often the offspring of a deity (god) and mortal

F. one hundred years

G. a solid containing water in which the molecular ratio of water to anhydrous compound is 1:2

H. existing, living, going without others

I. the base unit in mass; equal to 1,000 grams

J. an insect with supposedly 1,000 legs

## Definitions

**Directions:** Define the words below. The word in italics is fabricated.

1. multilingual _____

_____

2. equilateral _____

_____

3. *semilunar* _____

_____

4. soliloquy _____

_____

5. millennium _____

_____

# Unit 6 *(cont.)*

## Affix Practice

**Directions:** Fill in the blanks as directed. A sample has been given. List only one verb, adjective, etc. You may not find one of each.

Word: _____ intrude _____

Root Element: _____ trud _____     **Meaning:** _____ to thrust _____

Affix Element: _____ in _____     **Meaning:** _____ in, into _____

| Verb | Adjective | Adverb | Noun |
|------|-----------|--------|------|
| intrude | intrusive | intrusively | intruder, intrusion |

Word: _____ omnivore _____

Root Element: _____ vor _____     **Meaning:** _____ to devour _____

Affix Element: _____     **Meaning:** _____

| Verb | Adjective | Adverb | Noun |
|------|-----------|--------|------|
|  |  |  |  |

## Extended Activity

**Extra Words:** solitaire

**Definition:** any of a number of card games played by one person

**Directions:** Answer these questions.

➤ Do you like playing solitaire? Why or why not?

_____

_____

➤ What are some of your other favorite card games? _____

_____

_____

# Unit 6 Quiz

## Word Roots

**Directions:** Identify the root and write it on the first line. On the next, tell what the root means. Then define the whole word on the last line.

1. **omnidirectional**
   Root: _____
   Root Meaning: _____
   Word Definition: _____

2. **equivalent**
   Root: _____
   Root Meaning: _____
   Word Definition: _____

3. **multitude**
   Root: _____
   Root Meaning: _____
   Word Definition: _____

4. **semisweet**
   Root: _____
   Root Meaning: _____
   Word Definition: _____

5. **solidarity**
   Root: _____
   Root Meaning: _____
   Word Definition: _____

6. **hemistich**
   Root: _____
   Root Meaning: _____
   Word Definition: _____

7. **milliliter**
   Root: _____
   Root Meaning: _____
   Word Definition: _____

8. **kiloton**
   Root: _____
   Root Meaning: _____
   Word Definition: _____

9. **centigrade**
   Root: _____
   Root Meaning: _____
   Word Definition: _____

10. **demirelief**
    Root: _____
    Root Meaning: _____
    Word Definition: _____

## Matching

**Directions:** Match each word to its definition.

_____ 11. milliary

_____ 12. omnibus

_____ 13. equipollent

_____ 14. demirep

_____ 15. hemialgia

_____ 16. centipede

_____ 17. solely

_____ 18. semi-independent

_____ 19. multitudinous

_____ 20. kilocuries

A. pain afflicting half the body

B. equal to a Roman mile; 1,000 paces

C. alone, singly

D. 1,000 curies (radioactivity unit)

E. a list of all an author's writings

F. arthropod with one hundred feet

G. equal in force or power

H. someone of doubtful reputation

I. having many parts; existing in great numbers

J. partially dependent

**HEMINGWAY**

The Sun Also Rises
A Farewell to Arms
For Whom the Bell Tolls
The Old Man and the Sea
Islands in the Stream

# Unit 7

| Word Part | Meaning | Word Part | Meaning |
|---|---|---|---|
| aqu(a)- | water | -duc(t)- | lead |
| dict- | to say, speak | mal- | bad |
| capit- | head | -scrib, script- | write |
| carn- | flesh | spec-, spic- | look, see |
| corp- | body | circum- | around |
| val- | farewell | | |

## Matching

_____ 1. aquarium

_____ 2. aqueduct

_____ 3. capital

_____ 4. carnation

_____ 5. circumscribe

_____ 6. corpse

_____ 7. description

_____ 8. maledictions

_____ 9. spectacles

_____ 10. valedictorian

A. "written down"; an adjective gives this

B. eyeglasses

C. a dead body

D. curses; "bad speech"

E. to "write around"

F. a pink or flesh-colored flower

G. head city; seat of government

H. a structure that leads water

I. the person who delivers a farewell (usually at a graduation)

J. an enclosure used for fish; other sea creatures

## Definitions

**Directions:** Define the words below. The word in italics is fabricated.

1. *aquapolis* _____

_____

2. circumspect _____

_____

3. decapitation _____

_____

4. chili con carne _____

_____

5. Dictaphone _____

_____

# Unit 7 (cont.)

## Affix Practice

**Directions:** Fill in the blanks as directed. If needed, refer to the sample given on page 11. List only one verb, adjective, etc. You may not find one of each.

**Word:** _____predict_____

**Root Element:** _____dict_____   **Meaning:** ___to say, speak___

**Affix Element:** _____   **Meaning:** _____

| Verb | Adjective | Adverb | Noun |
|------|-----------|--------|------|
|      |           |        |      |

## Extended Activity

**Extra Word:** manuscript

**Definition:** a book, document, or other composition written by hand

**Directions:** The prefix in the word *manuscript* is *manu*. Starting with the word *manuscript*, create a word tree like the one with the word *kilometer* on page 6. You may be surprised how many words you know.

**Word 1:** manuscript
**Definition:** _____
_____

**Word 2A:** _____
**Definition:** _____
_____

**Word 2B:** _____
**Definition:** _____
_____

**Word 3A:** _____
**Definition:** _____
_____
_____

**Word 3B:** _____
**Definition:** _____
_____
_____

**Word 3C:** _____
**Definition:** _____
_____
_____

# Unit 7 Quiz

## Word Roots

**Directions:** Identify the root and write it on the first line. On the next, tell what the root means. Then define the whole word on the last line.

1. **dictator**
   Root: _____
   Root Meaning: _____
   Word Definition: _____

2. **viaduct**
   Root: _____
   Root Meaning: _____
   Word Definition: _____

3. **circumvent**
   Root: _____
   Root Meaning: _____
   Word Definition: _____

4. **aquacade**
   Root: _____
   Root Meaning: _____
   Word Definition: _____

5. **recapitulate**
   Root: _____
   Root Meaning: _____
   Word Definition: _____

6. **malady**
   Root: _____
   Root Meaning: _____
   Word Definition: _____

7. **reincarnation**
   Root: _____
   Root Meaning: _____
   Word Definition: _____

8. **prescribe**
   Root: _____
   Root Meaning: _____
   Word Definition: _____

9. **corporal**
   Root: _____
   Root Meaning: _____
   Word Definition: _____

10. **retrospect**
    Root: _____
    Root Meaning: _____
    Word Definition: _____

# Unit 7 Quiz *(cont.)*

## Matching

**Directions:** Match each word to its definition.

_____ 11. manuscript

_____ 12. benediction

_____ 13. capitol

_____ 14. corpus delicti

_____ 15. malodorous

_____ 16. perspective

_____ 17. conduct

_____ 18. carnivorous

_____ 19. subaqueous

_____ 20. circumference

A. marked by a bad odor

B. leading together

C. line around the circle

D. under the water

E. written by hand

F. flesh-eating

G. viewpoint; complete outlook

H. the main element of a crime (literally, "the body of a crime")

I. the building that houses the heads of government

J. to speak well

# Unit 8

| Word Part | Meaning | Word Part | Meaning |
|---|---|---|---|
| gyn- | woman | pat(er)- | father |
| ped- | child | mat(er)- | mother |
| card- | heart | frater- | brother |
| amor- | love | soror- | sister |
| the- | god | vir- | man |

## Matching

_____ 1. amorous

_____ 2. cardiogenic

_____ 3. fraternize

_____ 4. matriarch

_____ 5. misogyny

_____ 6. paternity

_____ 7. pediatrics

_____ 8. polytheism

_____ 9. sorority

_____ 10. virtue

A. moral excellence; goodness

B. fatherhood; authorship, origin

C. originating in the heart

D. chiefly social organization of college women

E. belief in more than one god

F. of or associated with love

G. a woman who rules a family

H. the branch of medicine that deals with the care and treatment of children

I. to associate with others in a brotherly way

J. hatred of women

## Definitions

**Directions:** Define the words below. Use a dictionary, if necessary.

1. triumvirate_____

_____

2. cardiograph_____

_____

3. pedagogue _____

_____

4. theocracy _____

_____

5. patricide _____

_____

# Unit 8 (cont.)

## Affix Practice

**Directions:** Fill in the blanks as directed. A sample has been given. List only one verb, adjective, etc. You may not find one of each.

**Word:** _____ intrude _____

**Root Element:** _____ trud _____     **Meaning:** _____ to thrust _____

**Affix Element:** _____ in _____     **Meaning:** _____ in, into _____

| Verb | Adjective | Adverb | Noun |
|------|-----------|--------|------|
| intrude | intrusive | intrusively | intruder, intrusion |

**Word:** _____ maternal _____

**Root Element:** _____ mat(er) _____     **Meaning:** _____ mother _____

**Affix Element:** _____ none _____     **Meaning:** _____ none _____

| Verb | Adjective | Adverb | Noun |
|------|-----------|--------|------|
|  |  |  |  |

## Extended Activity

**Extra Words:** matron of honor

**Definition:** a married woman serving as chief attendant of the bride at the wedding

**Directions:** Answer these questions:

➤ What is the name for the unmarried woman who serves as the attendant of the bride?

_____

_____

➤ How is a fraternal twin different than other twins? _____

_____

# Unit 8 Quiz

## Word Roots

**Directions**: Identify the root and write it on the first line. On the next line, tell what the root means. Then define the whole word on the last line.

1. **pedodontics**
   Root: _____
   Root Meaning: _____
   Word Definition: _____

2. **enamored**
   Root: _____
   Root Meaning: _____
   Word Definition: _____

3. **matrilocal**
   Root: _____
   Root Meaning: _____
   Word Definition: _____

4. **virtuoso**
   Root: _____
   Root Meaning: _____
   Word Definition: _____

5. **sororate**
   Root: _____
   Root Meaning: _____
   Word Definition: _____

6. **gynecologist**
   Root: _____
   Root Meaning: _____
   Word Definition: _____

7. **fraternization**
   Root: _____
   Root Meaning: _____
   Word Definition: _____

8. **patriarch**
   Root: _____
   Root Meaning: _____
   Word Definition: _____

9. **monotheism**
   Root: _____
   Root Meaning: _____
   Word Definition: _____

10. **cardiac arrest**
    Root: _____
    Root Meaning: _____
    Word Definition: _____

# Unit 8 Quiz (cont.)

## Matching

**Directions:** Match each word to its definition.

_____ 11. gynarchy          _____ 16. patristics

_____ 12. pedology          _____ 17. matrimony

_____ 13. cardiomyopathy    _____ 18. fratricide

_____ 14. amoretto          _____ 19. sororal

_____ 15. theomachy         _____ 20. virile

A. killing one's brother

B. a disease of the heart muscle

C. government by women

D. the study of children's physical and mental development

E. marriage

F. sisterly; resembling a sister

G. a cupid

H. manly; masculine

I. writings of the church fathers

J. strife or battle among gods

# Units 5–8 Review

**Directions:** Match the definitions on page 49 to the words below.

_____ 1. aquamarine

_____ 2. ascribe

_____ 3. bigamy

_____ 4. capitol

_____ 5. carnival

_____ 6. centennial

_____ 7. circumlocution

_____ 8. confraternity

_____ 9. conspicuous

_____ 10. corpuscle

_____ 11. December

_____ 12. demigod

_____ 13. dioxide

_____ 14. dismal

_____ 15. duplex

_____ 16. enamor

_____ 17. ennead

_____ 18. equitable

_____ 19. hemisphere

_____ 20. heptameter

_____ 21. hexapod

_____ 22. kilowatt

_____ 23. matron

_____ 24. million

_____ 25. monologue

_____ 26. multicolored

_____ 27. nonagenarian

_____ 28. November

_____ 29. octave

_____ 30. omnibus

_____ 31. patronymic

_____ 32. pediatrics

_____ 33. pentathlon

_____ 34. pericardium

_____ 35. polygamy

_____ 36. prediction

_____ 37. production

_____ 38. quadruplets

_____ 39. quart

_____ 40. quintet

_____ 41. Scripture

_____ 42. semiconscious

_____ 43. septennial

_____ 44. solo

_____ 45. sororicide

_____ 46. spectator

_____ 47. tetragon

_____ 48. theogony

_____ 49. tricycle

_____ 50. triumvirate

_____ 51. uniform

_____ 52. valediction

# Units 5–8 Review *(cont.)*

## Definitions

A. a mythological being with more power than mortals, but less than gods

B. causing gloom or depression

C. government of three people

D. 1,000 watts

E. 9th month (of original Roman calendar)

F. partially conscious

G. an observer of an event

H. an association of persons united in a common purpose

I. to inspire with love; captivate

J. a person 90 years old or between 90 and 99 years of age

K. an age or period of 100 years

L. an act of bidding farewell; a speech made as a farewell

M. the killing of one's sister

N. a pale blue to light greenish blue color

O. having more than one wife at a time

P. marrying one person while still married to another; having "two marriages"

Q. easy to notice or see

R. to name after one's father

S. composition for an individual voice or instrument

T. a tone that is eight tones above or below another tone

U. a compound with two oxygen atoms per molecule

V. a married woman or widow, especially a mother of dignity, mature age, and social position

W. conforming to one principle or rule; consistent

X. twofold; double

Y. a thousand thousands

Z. an account of the god's origin and genealogy

AA. the membranous sac that encloses the heart

BB. a six-legged arthropod; an insect

CC. talking around a subject

DD. one of four offspring born in a single birth

EE. a three-wheeled vehicle

FF. a printed anthology of the works of one author; a list of all works

GG. an athletic contest made up of five track-and-field events

HH. a festival marked by fun and feast

II. a dramatic long speech made by one person

JJ. a group or set of nine

KK. a metrical unit consisting of seven feet

LL. a four-sided polygon; a quadrilateral

MM. the branch of medicine that deals with the care and treatment of children

NN. one fourth of a gallon

OO. to attribute to a specified cause, source, or origin

PP. an unattached body cell

QQ. half a sphere

RR. a composition of five voices or instruments

SS. the tenth month of the Roman calendar

TT. marked by fairness; impartiality

UU. occurring every seven years; happening seven times a year

VV. a sacred writing or book

WW. something foretold; predicted

XX. to lead forward

YY. a building where the state legislature meets

ZZ. having many colors

# Units 5–8 Quiz

## Matching, Part I

**Directions:** Match each word to its definition.

_____ 1. ennead

_____ 2. bigamy

_____ 3. carnival

_____ 4. hemisphere

_____ 5. December

_____ 6. monologue

_____ 7. enamor

_____ 8. octave

_____ 9. production

_____ 10. tetragon

_____ 11. septennial

_____ 12. patronymic

_____ 13. ascribe

_____ 14. corpuscle

_____ 15. matron

A. to name after one's father

B. a tone that is eight tones above or below another tone

C. marrying one person while still married to another; "two marriages"

D. an unattached body cell

E. a festival marked by fun and feast

F. a four-sided polygon; a quadrilateral

G. occurring every seven years; happening seven times a year

H. a married woman or widow, especially a mother of dignity, mature age, and established social position

I. a group or set of nine

J. to lead forward

K. 10th month (of original Roman calendar)

L. to inspire with love; captivate

M. half a sphere

N. a speech made by one person

O. to attribute to a specified cause, source, origin

## Matching, Part II

**Directions:** Match each word to its definition.

_____ 16. multicolored

_____ 17. quintet

_____ 18. spectator

_____ 19. hexapod

_____ 20. uniform

_____ 21. centennial

_____ 22. theogony

_____ 23. omnibus

_____ 24. nonagenarian

_____ 25. confraternity

A. an age or period of 100 years

B. an association of persons united in a common purpose; comradry

C. an observer of an event

D. a six-legged arthropod; an insect

E. having many colors

F. a person 90 years old or between 90-100 years of age

G. an account of the gods' origins and genealogy

H. conforming to one principle, rule; consistent

I. a printed anthology of the works of one author; a list of all works

J. a composition of five voices and instruments

## True or False

**Directions:** Put a **T** for **True** or an **F** for **False** on the line next to each statement.

_____ 26. *Aquamarine* is a pale blue to light greenish blue color.

_____ 27. *Capitol* is the head city or seat of government

_____ 28. *Pentathlon* is an athletic contest made up of six track and field events

_____ 29. *Dioxide* is a compound with two hydrogen atoms per molecule.

_____ 30. *Equitable* is marked by fairness, impartiality.

_____ 31. *Quadruplets* are four offspring born in a single birth.

_____ 32. *Circumlocution* is talking around a subject.

_____ 33. *Pediatrics* is the branch of medicine that deals with the care and treatment of the feet.

_____ 34. *Dismal* is causing depression and gloom.

_____ 35. *Kilowatt* is 1,000 watts.

## Fill in the Blank

**Directions:** Fill in the blank with the appropriate answer. Choose words from the box.

| | | | |
|---|---|---|---|
| conspicuous | November | quart | sororicide |
| demigod | pericardium | Scripture | tricycle |
| duplex | polygamy | semiconcious | triumvirate |
| heptameter | prediction | solo | valediction |
| million | | | |

36. _____ is a mythological being with more power than mortals but less than gods.

37. The man committed _____ because he had more than one wife at a time.

38. An act of bidding farewell or a speech made as a farewell is known as a _____.

39. A _____ person is someone who is easy to notice or see.

40. The membranous sac that encloses the heart is called the _____.

41. A _____ of milk is one-fourth of a gallon.

42. When Sylvia sang alone, her performance was called a _____.

43. _____ is the killing one's sister.

44. A _____ has three wheels.

45. Caesar, Brutus, and Cassias were a _____—a government of three people.

46. Twofold and double mean the same thing as _____.

47. A metrical unit consisting of seven feet is called a _____.

48. A _____ is a thousand thousands.

49. The ninth month of the Roman calendar is _____.

50. When a psychic is foretelling something to us, he/she is making a _____.

# Vocabulary List

| Word Part | Meaning |
|---|---|
| ann, enn | year |
| aud | sound, hearing |
| biblio | book |
| cede, ceed, cess | to go |
| cogn | learn |
| cosm | world, universe |
| cred | to believe |
| cryo | cold |
| derm | skin |
| dox | opinion, belief |
| eu | good, well |
| fac | to make, do |
| fid | faith |
| gog(ue) | ruler, leader |
| grad, gress | to move |
| hier | holy, sacred |
| homo | same |
| jac, ject | throw, hurl |
| lith | stone |
| loqu | to say, speak |
| lun | moon |

52

# Vocabulary List *(cont.)*

| Word Part | Meaning |
|---|---|
| macro | large, great |
| man(u) | hand |
| mar | sea |
| meso | middle |
| mis, mit | to send |
| nau | ship |
| port | to bring, carry |
| pro | forward |
| psych | mind |
| ques, qui(s) | to ask, seek |
| sens, sent | feel |
| sol | sun |
| spir | to breathe |
| temp | time |
| trans | across |
| verb | word |
| vor | to eat |
| zoo | animal |

# Unit 9

| Word Part | Meaning | Word Part | Meaning |
|---|---|---|---|
| psych- | mind | spir- | to breathe |
| loqu- | to say, speak | man(u)- | hand |
| biblio- | book | homo- | same |
| eu- | good, well | trans- | across |
| fac- | to make, do | -port- | to bring, carry |

## Matching

_____ 1. bibliophile

_____ 2. euphony

_____ 3. factory

_____ 4. homogeneous

_____ 5. manual

_____ 6. psychology

_____ 7. respiration

_____ 8. soliloquy

_____ 9. transcription

_____ 10. transport

A. the act of inhaling and exhaling; breathing

B. to carry from one place to another

C. a lover or collector of books

D. same or similar nature of kind of something

E. thoughts or feelings of a character spoken when alone

F. agreeable sound

G. a full written copy; "write across"

H. a building where things are made

I. the study of mental processes and behavior

J. done by, used by, operated by hands

## Definitions

**Directions:** Define the words below.

1. psychopath _____

_____

2. bibliography _____

_____

3. spirometer _____

_____

4. homonym _____

_____

5. eulogy _____

_____

## Affix Practice

**Directions:** Fill in the blanks as directed. Use previous worksheets as examples, if needed.

**Word:** _____ important _____

**Root Element:** _____ port _____    **Meaning:** _____ to bring, carry _____

**Affix Element:** _____    **Meaning:** _____

| Verb | Adjective | Adverb | Noun |
|------|-----------|--------|------|
|      |           |        |      |

## Extended Activity

**Extra Word:** ventriloquist

**Definition:** a person who projects his/her voice so that it seems to come from another source

**Directions:** Answer this question:

❏ Can you name any famous ventriloquists? Name their dummies, too, if you can.

_____

_____

_____

# Unit 9 Quiz

## Word Roots

**Directions:** Identify the root and write it on the first line. On the next, tell what the root means. Then define the whole word on the last line.

1. **bibliomania**
   Root: _____
   Root Meaning: _____
   Word Definition: _____

2. **homogenize**
   Root: _____
   Root Meaning: _____
   Word Definition: _____

3. **manacle**
   Root: _____
   Root Meaning: _____
   Word Definition: _____

4. **euphemism**
   Root: _____
   Root Meaning: _____
   Word Definition: _____

5. **deportation**
   Root: _____
   Root Meaning: _____
   Word Definition: _____

6. **factual**
   Root: _____
   Root Meaning: _____
   Word Definition: _____

7. **ventriloquist**
   Root: _____
   Root Meaning: _____
   Word Definition: _____

8. **psychiatry**
   Root: _____
   Root Meaning: _____
   Word Definition: _____

9. **inspiration**
   Root: _____
   Root Meaning: _____
   Word Definition: _____

10. **translucent**
    Root: _____
    Root Meaning: _____
    Word Definition: _____

# Unit 9 Quiz *(cont.)*

## Matching

**Directions:** Match each word to its definition.

_____ 11. eulogy

_____ 12. facsimile

_____ 13. soliloquy

_____ 14. psychedelic

_____ 15. perspire

_____ 16. biblioklept

_____ 17. portfolio

_____ 18. transcontinental

_____ 19. homophone

_____ 20. manicure

A. positive words spoken about a deceased person

B. spanning or crossing a continent

C. marked with hallucinations, mental distortions

D. having the same sound but different spelling, origin, meaning

E. thoughts or feelings of a character spoken when alone

F. the care of hands and fingernails

G. something made similar; reproduction, copy

H. "breathing through the skin"

I. a person who steals books

J. a flat carrying case that holds papers

# Unit 10

| Word Part | Meaning | Word Part | Meaning |
|---|---|---|---|
| sens-, sent- | feel | temp- | time |
| mis-, mit- | send | jac-, ject- | throw, hurl |
| fid- | faith | derm- | skin |
| gog(ue)- | ruler, leader | dox- | opinion, belief |
| pro- | forward | grad-, gress- | to move |

## Matching

_____ 1. adjacent

_____ 2. confidant

_____ 3. demagogue

_____ 4. epidermis

_____ 5. graduation

_____ 6. heterodox

_____ 7. interject

_____ 8. progress

_____ 9. temporary

_____ 10. transmit

A. close to, "thrown" near

B. the outer protective layer of skin

C. a leader of the people (usually a bad one)

D. to send; to spread across

E. one to whom secrets or private matters are told

F. receipt of academic degree or diploma upon completion of studies

G. not in agreement with accepted opinion or belief

H. movement toward a goal; moving forward

I. lasting for a limited time

J. to throw between

## Definitions

**Directions:** Define the words below.

1. intermission _____

_____

2. hypodermic _____

_____

3. pedagogue _____

_____

4. doxology _____

_____

5. sentiment _____

_____

# Unit 10 *(cont.)*

## Affix Practice

**Directions:** Fill in the blanks as directed. Use previous worksheets as examples, if needed.

**Word:** _____ dissension _____

**Root Element:** _____ sent _____   **Meaning:** _____ feel _____

**Affix Element:** _____   **Meaning:** _____

| Verb | Adjective | Adverb | Noun |
|------|-----------|--------|------|
|      |           |        |      |

## Extended Activity

**Extra Word:** affidavit

**Definition:** a written declaration made under oath before an authorized official.

**Directions:** There are several words of law that are derived from Latin and Greek roots. Find the origins and meanings of the following words.

1. **amicus curiae**

   Origin: _____

   Meaning: _____

2. **corpus delecti**

   Origin: _____

   Meaning: _____

3. **ex post facto**

   Origin: _____

   Meaning: _____

# Unit 10 Quiz

## Word Roots

**Directions:** Identify the root and write it on the first line. On the next, tell what the root means. Then define the whole word on the last line.

1. **infidel**
   Root: _____
   Root Meaning: _____
   Word Definition: _____

2. **orthodox**
   Root: _____
   Root Meaning: _____
   Word Definition: _____

3. **hypnagogic**
   Root: _____
   Root Meaning: _____
   Word Definition: _____

4. **permit**
   Root: _____
   Root Meaning: _____
   Word Definition: _____

5. **proclaim**
   Root: _____
   Root Meaning: _____
   Word Definition: _____

6. **ectoderm**
   Root: _____
   Root Meaning: _____
   Word Definition: _____

7. **adjacent**
   Root: _____
   Root Meaning: _____
   Word Definition: _____

8. **gradual**
   Root: _____
   Root Meaning: _____
   Word Definition: _____

9. **insensitive**
   Root: _____
   Root Meaning: _____
   Word Definition: _____

10. **tempo**
    Root: _____
    Root Meaning: _____
    Word Definition: _____

## Matching

**Directions:** Match each word to its definition.

_____ 11. dermatitis

_____ 12. confidant

_____ 13. paradox

_____ 14. project

_____ 15. synagogue

_____ 16. transgression

_____ 17. missionary

_____ 18. sentimental

_____ 19. remit

_____ 20. contemporary

A. a person living during the same time period as another

B. to throw forward

C. a place for Jewish worship, leadership

D. skin rash

E. appealing to emotions, feelings

F. one sent to do religious work

G. a person in which one has faith

H. to send (money)

I. opinion, belief that appears to contradict itself

J. to go beyond or over a limit

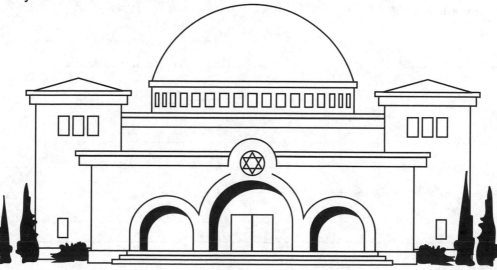

# Unit 11

| Word Part | Meaning | Word Part | Meaning |
|---|---|---|---|
| nau- | ship | mar- | sea |
| lun- | moon | ann-, enn- | year |
| sol- | sun | lith- | stone |
| cred- | to believe | verb- | word |
| zoo- | animal | | |

## Matching

_____ 1. accredited

_____ 2. anniversary

_____ 3. lithography

_____ 4. lunatic

_____ 5. maritime

_____ 6. nausea

_____ 7. perennial

_____ 8. solstice

_____ 9. verbosity

_____ 10. zoology

A. a printing process in which the image is printed on a flat surface, like stone

B. either of two times when the sun is the farthest distance from the celestial equator

C. a feeling of sickness in the stomach; seasickness

D. insane; a person affected by the moon

E. the branch of biology that deals with animals

F. the use of an excessive amount of words

G. to supply with credentials; authorized

H. lasting through the year or through many years

I. the annual recurring date of a past event

J. of, relating to, adjacent to the sea

## Definitions

**Directions**: Define the words below. The words in italics are fabricated.

1. astronaut _____

_____

2. monolith _____

_____

3. *demilune* _____

_____

4. *zoography* _____

_____

5. submarine _____

_____

# Unit 11 (cont.)

## Affix Practice

**Directions:** Fill in the blanks as directed. Use previous worksheets as examples, if needed.

**Word:** _____ incredible _____

**Root Element:** _____ cred _____    **Meaning:** _____ to believe _____

**Affix Element:** _____    **Meaning:** _____

| Verb | Adjective | Adverb | Noun |
|------|-----------|--------|------|
|      |           |        |      |

## Extended Activity

**Extra Word:** mermaid

**Definition:** a legendary sea creature having the head and upper body of a woman and the tail of a fish. *Mer* is a variation of *mar*.

**Directions:** Answer these questions:

➤ What do you call a legendary sea creature that is part man and part fish?

_____

➤ Can you think of any mermaids from movies, television shows, or books? Name as many works of art as you can that have mermaids as characters in them.

_____

_____

_____

# Unit 11 Quiz

## Word Roots

**Directions:** Identify the root and write it on the first line.  On the next, tell what the root means.  Then define the whole word on the last line.

1. **lunatic**
   Root: _____
   Root Meaning: _____
   Word Definition: _____

2. **discreditable**
   Root: _____
   Root Meaning: _____
   Word Definition: _____

3. **aquamarine**
   Root: _____
   Root Meaning: _____
   Word Definition: _____

4. **lithographic**
   Root: _____
   Root Meaning: _____
   Word Definition: _____

5. **semiannual**
   Root: _____
   Root Meaning: _____
   Word Definition: _____

6. **bicentennial**
   Root: _____
   Root Meaning: _____
   Word Definition: _____

7. **solar system**
   Root: _____
   Root Meaning: _____
   Word Definition: _____

8. **verbatim**
   Root: _____
   Root Meaning: _____
   Word Definition: _____

9. **nauseous**
   Root: _____
   Root Meaning: _____
   Word Definition: _____

10. **zoology**
    Root: _____
    Root Meaning: _____
    Word Definition: _____

# Unit 11 Quiz *(cont.)*

## Matching

**Directions:** Match each word to its definition.

_____ 11. annuity                    _____ 16. verbivore

_____ 12. nautical                   _____ 17. zoology

_____ 13. Neolithic                  _____ 18. solarium

_____ 14. credentials                _____ 19. decade

_____ 15. lunar                      _____ 20. mariner

A. a sailor or seaman

B. a period of 10 years; every 10 years

C. the yearly payment of allowance or income

D. the branch of biology dealing with animals

E. a room exposed to the sun

F. written proof or evidence of qualification

G. of or relating to sailors or ships

H. a period around 10,000 B.C. characterized by the making of advanced stone tools

I. of or pertaining to the moon

J. a devourer of words

# Unit 12

| Word Part | Meaning | Word Part | Meaning |
|-----------|---------|-----------|---------|
| meso- | middle | cede-, ceed-, cess- | to go |
| macro- | large, great | cosm- | world, universe |
| cogn- | learn | hier- | holy, sacred |
| cryo- | cold | aud- | sound, hearing |
| ques-, qui(s)- | ask, seek | vor- | to eat |

## Matching

_____ 1. carnivore

_____ 2. cryosurgery

_____ 3. hierarchy

_____ 4. inaudible

_____ 5. incognito

_____ 6. inquisitive

_____ 7. macrography

_____ 8. Mesopotamia

_____ 9. microcosm

_____ 10. precede

A. a flesh-eating animal

B. to come, exist, or occur before in time

C. the selective exposure of tissues to extreme cold

D. a small representative system having analogies to a larger configuration

E. religious rule by a group of ranked clergy; one of the divisions of angels

F. an ancient region of southwest Asia settled before 5,000 B.C.

G. impossible to hear

H. unusually large handwriting

I. with one's identity concealed or disguised

J. curious; asking questions

## Definitions

**Directions:** Define the words below. The word in italics is fabricated.

1. omnivore _____

   _____

2. mesoderm _____

   _____

3. *hierocracy* _____

   _____

4. macrocosm _____

   _____

5. audience _____

   _____

# Unit 12 *(cont.)*

## Affix Practice

**Directions:** Fill in the blanks as directed.  Use previous worksheets for example, if needed.

**Word:** _____ recession _____

**Root Element:** _____ cess _____     **Meaning:** _____ to go _____

**Affix Element:** _____     **Meaning:** _____

| Verb | Adjective | Adverb | Noun |
|------|-----------|--------|------|
|      |           |        |      |

## Extended Activity

**Extra Word:** precognition

**Definition:**  act of knowing ahead of time

**Directions:**  Answer these questions:

➣ Has there been a time you have experienced precognition?

_____

_____

➣ How might you benefit from having precognition? _____

_____

➣ Can you think of times when it would be undesirable to have precognition?

_____

_____

# Unit 12 Quiz

## Word Roots

**Directions:** Identify the root and write it on the first line. On the next, tell what the root means. Then define the whole word on the last line.

1. **cryosurgery**
   Root: _____
   Root Meaning: _____
   Word Definition: _____

2. **mesosphere**
   Root: _____
   Root Meaning: _____
   Word Definition: _____

3. **excessive**
   Root: _____
   Root Meaning: _____
   Word Definition: _____

4. **auditorium**
   Root: _____
   Root Meaning: _____
   Word Definition: _____

5. **cosmopolitan**
   Root: _____
   Root Meaning: _____
   Word Definition: _____

6. **precognition**
   Root: _____
   Root Meaning: _____
   Word Definition: _____

7. **inquest**
   Root: _____
   Root Meaning: _____
   Word Definition: _____

8. **hieroglyphics**
   Root: _____
   Root Meaning: _____
   Word Definition: _____

9. **macrophage**
   Root: _____
   Root Meaning: _____
   Word Definition: _____

10. **herbivore**
    Root: _____
    Root Meaning: _____
    Word Definition: _____

## Matching

**Directions:** Match each word to its definition.

_____ 11. macroscopic

_____ 12. Mesolithic

_____ 13. hieratic

_____ 14. inquisition

_____ 15. cognizance

_____ 16. cosmonaut

_____ 17. cryogen

_____ 18. audiophile

_____ 19. proceed

_____ 20. voracious

A. an investigation; interrogation

B. one who loves sound

C. a refrigerant that produces low temperatures

D. of or relating to the middle Stone Age period

E. to continue; to go forward

F. consuming or eating great amounts of food

G. a space traveler

H. large enough to be seen by the naked eye

I. conscious knowledge; observance

J. of or relating to sacred or holy offices

# Units 9–12 Review

**Directions:** Match the definitions on page 71 to the words below.

| | |
|---|---|
| _____ 1. factory | _____ 26. paradox |
| _____ 2. confidant | _____ 27. proceed |
| _____ 3. remit | _____ 28. precede |
| _____ 4. homogeneous | _____ 29. interject |
| _____ 5. graduation | _____ 30. manicure |
| _____ 6. bibliophile | _____ 31. contemporary |
| _____ 7. perennial | _____ 32. facsimile |
| _____ 8. progress | _____ 33. demagogue |
| _____ 9. temporary | _____ 34. adjacent |
| _____ 10. perspire | _____ 35. epidermis |
| _____ 11. accredited | _____ 36. heterodox |
| _____ 12. euphony | _____ 37. lunatic |
| _____ 13. psychology | _____ 38. microcosm |
| _____ 14. respiration | _____ 39. audiophile |
| _____ 15. maritime | _____ 40. project |
| _____ 16. transmit | _____ 41. eulogy |
| _____ 17. verbosity | _____ 42. sentimental |
| _____ 18. manual | _____ 43. homophone |
| _____ 19. transcription | _____ 44. psychedelic |
| _____ 20. inaudible | _____ 45. transcontinental |
| _____ 21. nausea | _____ 46. zoology |
| _____ 22. anniversary | _____ 47. carnivore |
| _____ 23. incognito | _____ 48. inquisitive |
| _____ 24. soliloquy | _____ 49. voracious |
| _____ 25. cognizance | _____ 50. transport |

## Definitions

A. the act of inhaling and exhaling; breathing

B. the study of mental processes and behavior

C. a feeling of sickness in the stomach; seasickness

D. insane; a person affected by the moon

E. appealing to emotions, feelings

F. agreeable sound

G. conscious knowledge; observance

H. a building where things are made

I. spanning or crossing a continent

J. unduly curious and seeking knowledge

K. of, relating to, adjacent to the sea

L. movement toward a goal; moving forward

M. a lover or collector of books

N. a full written copy; "write across"

O. the branch of biology that deals with animals

P. done by, used by, operated by hands

Q. a flesh-eating animal

R. to come, exist, or occur before in time

S. the annual recurring date of a past event

T. to continue; to go forward

U. receipt of academic degree or diploma upon completion of studies

V. to send; to spread across

W. one to whom secrets or private matters are told

X. a small representative system having analogies to a larger configuration

Y. lasting through the year or through many years

Z. the use of an excessive amount of words

AA. to supply with credentials; authorized

BB. to carry from one place to another

CC. one who loves sound

DD. same or similar nature of kind of something

EE. thoughts or feelings of a character spoken when alone

FF. consuming or eating great amounts of food

GG. not in agreement with accepted opinion or belief

HH. impossible to hear

II. with one's identity concealed or disguised

JJ. lasting for a limited time

KK. to throw between

LL. the outer protective layer of skin

MM. a leader of the people

NN. close to, "thrown" near

OO. marked with hallucinations, mental distortions

PP. having the same sound but different spelling, origin, meaning

QQ. something made similar; reproduction, copy

RR. sweat (literally, "breathe through")

SS. to send (money)

TT. a person living during the same time period as another

UU. to throw forward

VV. opinion, belief that appears to contradict itself

WW. positive words spoken about a deceased person

XX. the care of hands and fingernails

# Vocabulary List

| Word Part | Meaning |
|---|---|
| ailuro | cats |
| andr | men |
| arachn(o) | spiders |
| cyno | dogs |
| eco | house |
| ento | insects |
| etymo(s) | true, real |
| icthyo | fish |
| kines(io) | movement |
| meteor(on) | weather |
| muri | mice, rodents |
| neo | new |
| numero | number |
| ophthalmo | eye |
| ornitho | birds |
| osteo | bones |
| paleo | ancient |
| pharma | drugs |
| tauto | the same |

# Unit 13

## Affix Practice

**Directions:** Listed below are three kinds of words parts: prefixes, roots, and suffixes. Form 20 words by combining any two or three word parts. Then list the words' definitions. An example is given below. Use an extra sheet of paper, if necessary.

### Prefixes

**ad:** toward, near

**de:** reverse

**dis:** against, opposite

**in:** not, in, into, within

**inter:** between

**intro:** inward

**per:** containing a large proportion

**pre:** before

**pro:** forward

**re:** back, again

### Roots

**cede, ceed, cess:** to go

**cred:** to believe

**duc(t):** to lead

**ject:** to throw

**mit, mis:** to send

**scrip(t), scrib:** to write

**spec, spic:** to look, see

### Suffixes

**able, ible:** capable of

**ate:** having, characterized by; to act upon

**ion:** action or process

**ive:** tending toward a specified action

**or, er:** one who performs

| Words | Meanings |
|---|---|
| inspection | the act or process of looking in something |

# Unit 14

| Word Part | Meaning | Word Part | Meaning |
|-----------|---------|-----------|---------|
| -phobia | fear of | andr- | men |
| ornitho- | birds | ailuro- | cats |
| arachn(o)- | spiders | cyno- | dogs |
| ento- | insects | icthyo- | fish |
| muri- | mice, rodents | pharma- | drugs |

## Matching

**Directions:**

Match the words to their definitions. You won't find many of these in your dictionary. (Note: Two words will share the same answers.)

_____ 1. ailurophobia
_____ 2. androphobia
_____ 3. anthropophobia
_____ 4. aquaphobia
_____ 5. arachnophobia
_____ 6. bibliophobia
_____ 7. chronophobia
_____ 8. cynophobia
_____ 9. demophobia
_____ 10. entophobia
_____ 11. gamophobia
_____ 12. gynephobia
_____ 13. heliophobia
_____ 14. hydrophobia
_____ 15. icthyophobia
_____ 16. maledictaphobia
_____ 17. monophobia
_____ 18. muriphobia
_____ 19. ornithophobia
_____ 20. pathophobia
_____ 21. pedophobia
_____ 22. pharmacophobia
_____ 23. philophobia
_____ 24. photophobia
_____ 25. pyrophobia
_____ 26. scriptophobia
_____ 27. sophophobia
_____ 28. theophobia
_____ 29. thermophobia
_____ 30. verbaphobia

*fear of . . .*
A. God, gods
B. mankind
C. drugs
D. marriage
E. being alone
F. water
G. cats
H. light
I. heat
J. fish
K. women
L. time
M. dogs
N. love
O. fire
P. words
Q. mice
R. spiders
S. people
T. sun
U. writing
V. disease
W. books
X. birds
Y. bad words
Z. insects
AA. knowledge, wisdom
BB. men
CC. children

# Unit 15

| Word Part | Meaning | Word Part | Meaning |
|-----------|---------|-----------|---------|
| -logy | study of | meteor(on)- | weather |
| etymo(s)- | true, real | paleo- | ancient |
| numero- | number | osteo- | bones |
| tauto- | the same | eco- | house |
| kines(io) | movement | opthalmo- | eye |
| neo- | new | | |

## Matching

**Directions:**

Match the words to their definitions. You won't find many of these in your dictionary.

| | | _study of . . ._ |
|---|---|---|
| _____ | 1. anthropology | A. skin |
| _____ | 2. archeology | B. birds |
| _____ | 3. astrology | C. opinions, beliefs |
| _____ | 4. audiology | D. bones |
| _____ | 5. biology | E. life |
| _____ | 6. cardiology | F. ancient forms, fossils |
| _____ | 7. chronology | G. fish |
| _____ | 8. dermatology | H. repetition of words |
| _____ | 9. doxology | I. mind, emotions, behavior |
| _____ | 10. ecology | J. the heart |
| _____ | 11. etymology | K. true meanings of words |
| _____ | 12. eulogy | L. good, well wishes |
| _____ | 13. genealogy | M. hearing, sound |
| _____ | 14. geology | N. new words |
| _____ | 15. graphology | O. ancestry, birth, kind |
| _____ | 16. ichthyology | P. human movement |
| _____ | 17. kinesiology | Q. organisms and where they live |
| _____ | 18. meteorology | R. Earth |
| _____ | 19. neology | S. time |
| _____ | 20. numerology | T. stars |
| _____ | 21. ornithology | U. handwriting |
| _____ | 22. ophthalmology | V. weather |
| _____ | 23. osteology | W. the past through artifacts |
| _____ | 24. paleontology | X. mankind |
| _____ | 25. philology | Y. God, gods |
| _____ | 26. psychology | Z. numbers |
| _____ | 27. tautology | AA. eyes |
| _____ | 28. theology | BB. love |

# Unit 16

## Word Trees

**Directions:** Refer to the word tree worksheet on page 6 to fill out the chart below. Start with one word from the box. Then think of two other words based on a part from that word. Next, think of three more words based on those two. Write definitions on the lines.

| | | |
|---|---|---|
| underneath | decimeter | astronaut |
| biology | aqueduct | carnivore |
| monarchy | cardiogenic | hierarchy |
| telephone | bibliophile | gamophobia |
| synchronize | pedagogue | audiology |
| biennial | | |

**Word 1:** _____

**Definition:** _____

_____

**Word 2A:** _____

**Definition:** _____

_____

**Word 2B:** _____

**Definition:** _____

_____

**Word 3A:** _____

**Definition:** _____

_____

_____

**Word 3B:** _____

**Definition:** _____

_____

_____

**Word 3C:** _____

**Definition:** _____

_____

_____

## Word Trees *(cont.)*

**Directions:** Refer to the word tree worksheet on page 6 to fill out the chart below. Start with one word from the box. Then think of two other words based on a part from that word. Next, think of three more words based on those two. Write definitions on the lines underneath.

| | | |
|---|---|---|
| geography | circumspect | microcosm |
| pathology | polytheism | thermophobia |
| periscope | transport | psychology |
| pentagon | hypodermic | anthropology |
| millipede | zoology | |

**Word 1:** _____
**Definition:** _____
_____

**Word 2A:** _____
**Definition:** _____
_____

**Word 2B:** _____
**Definition:** _____
_____

**Word 3A:** _____
**Definition:** _____
_____

**Word 3B:** _____
**Definition:** _____
_____

**Word 3C:** _____
**Definition:** _____
_____

# Vocabulary List

| Word Part | Meaning |
|---|---|
| ambi, amphi | both |
| anim | life, spirit |
| belli | war |
| cad, cid | to fall |
| chrom | color |
| clam, claim | to cry out |
| clud, claus | shut, close |
| cycl | circle |
| dia | across, through |
| doc(t) | to teach |
| ego | self, I |
| epi | on, upon |
| err | to wander |
| fall | to deceive |
| flam | fire |
| flor | flower |
| gon | corner, angle |
| herb | plant |
| hetero | other, another |
| iatr | healing |
| medi | middle |

# Vocabulary List *(cont.)*

| Word Part | Meaning |
|---|---|
| mne | to remember |
| morph | form, shape |
| nat | to be born |
| ortho | straight |
| pend | to hang, weigh |
| post | after |
| rect | straight |
| retro | backward |
| scend | to climb |
| simil, simul | same, like |
| soma | body, flesh |
| sub | under, below |
| super | above, beyond |
| techni | skill, craft |
| terr | earth |
| vid, vis | to see |
| voc | to call out |
| vol | wish |

# Unit 17

| Word Part | Meaning | Word Part | Meaning |
|---|---|---|---|
| hetero- | other, another | rect- | straight |
| pend- | to hang, weight | ego- | self, I |
| soma- | body, flesh | chrom- | color |
| iatr- | healing | techni- | skill, craft |
| vol- | wish | clam-, claim- | to cry out |

## Matching

_____ 1. architect

_____ 2. correct

_____ 3. egotist

_____ 4. heteronym

_____ 5. iatrogenic

_____ 6. malevolence

_____ 7. monochromatic

_____ 8. pendulum

_____ 9. proclamation

_____ 10. psychosomatic

A. a disorder with physical symptoms but originates from mental or emotional causes

B. healing induced by a physician's manner, activity, therapy

C. one who is devoted to his/her own interests and advancement

D. having only one color

E. one who designs and supervises construction of buildings

F. to remove the errors from; error-free

G. an announcement; a crying out

H. one of two or more words with identical spellings but different meanings and pronunciations

I. a body suspended from a fixed support that swings freely back and forth under the influence of gravity

J. the quality of wishing harm on someone

# Unit 17 *(cont.)*

## Definitions

**Directions:** Define the words below.

1. chromosome _____

   _____

2. benevolence _____

   _____

3. heterogeneous _____

   _____

4. podiatry _____

   _____

5. technology _____

   _____

## Affix Practice

**Directions:** Fill in the blanks as directed. Use previous worksheets as examples, if needed.

**Word:** _____ exclaim _____

**Root Element:** _____ claim _____     **Meaning:** _____ to cry out _____

**Affix Element:** _____     **Meaning:** _____

| Verb | Adjective | Adverb | Noun |
|------|-----------|--------|------|
|      |           |        |      |
|      |           |        |      |

## Extended Activity

➤ *Heteronym* was a word you were given in the Matching section on page 80. Please give as many examples of heteronyms as you can.

_____     _____     _____

_____     _____     _____

_____     _____     _____

# Unit 17 Quiz

## Word Roots

**Directions:** Identify the root and write it on the first line. On the next, tell what the root means. Then define the whole word on the last line.

1. **chromosphere**
   Root: _____
   Root Meaning: _____
   Word Definition: _____

2. **appendage**
   Root: _____
   Root Meaning: _____
   Word Definition: _____

3. **technical**
   Root: _____
   Root Meaning: _____
   Word Definition: _____

4. **pediatrics**
   Root: _____
   Root Meaning: _____
   Word Definition: _____

5. **volunteer**
   Root: _____
   Root Meaning: _____
   Word Definition: _____

6. **heterodox**
   Root: _____
   Root Meaning: _____
   Word Definition: _____

7. **direction**
   Root: _____
   Root Meaning: _____
   Word Definition: _____

8. **egocentric**
   Root: _____
   Root Meaning: _____
   Word Definition: _____

9. **somatogenic**
   Root: _____
   Root Meaning: _____
   Word Definition: _____

10. **reclamation**
    Root: _____
    Root Meaning: _____
    Word Definition: _____

# Unit 17 Quiz *(cont.)*

## Matching

**Directions:** Match each word to its definition.

_____ 11. rectify

_____ 12. egomania

_____ 13. geriatric

_____ 14. somatic

_____ 15. chromium

_____ 16. impending

_____ 17. volition

_____ 18. heterocyclic

_____ 19. disclaim

_____ 20. technique

A. a branch of medicine dealing with the problems and diseases of old age and aging

B. about to happen; hanging or suspended

C. to make or set right

D. containing different kinds of atoms joined together in a ring

E. to deny or disown

F. an excitement or enthusiasm induced by oneself

G. way or method in which something is done

H. a bluish-white metallic element used in alloys

I. pertaining to the body

J. choice, will

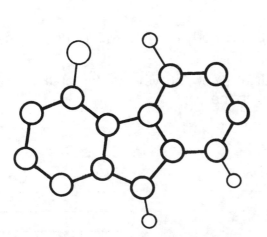

# Unit 18

| Word Part | Meaning | Word Part | Meaning |
|-----------|---------|-----------|---------|
| sub- | under, below | terr- | earth |
| post- | after | ortho- | straight |
| retro- | backward | epi- | on, upon |
| gon- | corner, angle | morph- | form, shape |
| vid-, vis- | to see | herb- | plant |

## Matching

_____ 1. epidermis

_____ 2. herbicide

_____ 3. invisible

_____ 4. morphology

_____ 5. octagon

_____ 6. orthodontist

_____ 7. postnatal

_____ 8. retrospect

_____ 9. submarine

_____ 10. terrarium

A. a small enclosure where land animals like turtles are kept

B. an eight-sided figure

C. impossible to see; not accessible by view

D. of or occurring after birth

E. the outer protective layer of skin

F. machine operating under water

G. a dental specialist who prevents and corrects irregularities of teeth

H. a substance used to kill plants (weeds)

I. the study of the forms of organisms

J. a review, survey, contemplation of things in the past

# Unit 18 *(cont.)*

## Definitions

**Directions:** Define the words below. The word in italics is fabricated.

1. subterranean _____

   _____

2. postgraduate_____

   _____

3. *retrodiction* _____

   _____

4. anthropomorphism _____

   _____

5. orthopedics_____

   _____

6. video_____

   _____

7. nonagon _____

   _____

8. herbivore_____

   _____

9. extraterrestrial_____

   _____

10. polymorphic _____

    _____

## Extended Activity

**Extra Word 1:** epitaph

**Definition:** an inscription on a tombstone in memory of the one buried there

➤ What would you want your tombstone to say about you? _____

_____

**Extra Word 2:** epithet

**Definition:** a term used as a descriptive substitute for a person's name or title, such as *The Great Emancipator* for Abraham Lincoln

➤ What would be an epithet that could be used for you? _____

# Unit 18 Quiz

## Word Roots

**Directions:** Identify the root and write it on the first line. On the next, tell what the root means. Then define the whole word on the last line.

1. **postpone**
   Root: _____
   Root Meaning: _____
   Word Definition: _____

2. **terrain**
   Root: _____
   Root Meaning: _____
   Word Definition: _____

3. **videlicet**
   Root: _____
   Root Meaning: _____
   Word Definition: _____

4. **herbage**
   Root: _____
   Root Meaning: _____
   Word Definition: _____

5. **diagonal**
   Root: _____
   Root Meaning: _____
   Word Definition: _____

6. **retrovirus**
   Root: _____
   Root Meaning: _____
   Word Definition: _____

7. **orthodontia**
   Root: _____
   Root Meaning: _____
   Word Definition: _____

8. **episode**
   Root: _____
   Root Meaning: _____
   Word Definition: _____

9. **morphologist**
   Root: _____
   Root Meaning: _____
   Word Definition: _____

10. **subsonic**
    Root: _____
    Root Meaning: _____
    Word Definition: _____

## Matching

**Directions:** Match each word to its definition.

_____ 11. retrograde

_____ 12. terra cotta

_____ 13. posthumous

_____ 14. metamorphosis

_____ 15. tetragon

_____ 16. epitaph

_____ 17. submerge

_____ 18. herbarium

_____ 19. orthography

_____ 20. visionary

A. a reddish brown earthenware

B. an inscription on a tombstone

C. to put under the surface of the water

D. spelling; "writing straight"

E. retreat; move back

F. one who sees vivid pictures from imagination, the future

G. a change in form

H. a four-sided figure

I. a collection of dried plants

J. occurring after death

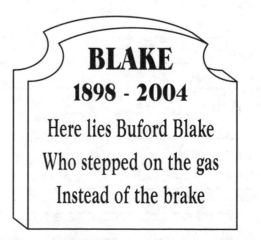

BLAKE

1898 - 2004

Here lies Buford Blake
Who stepped on the gas
Instead of the brake

# Unit 19

| Word Part | Meaning | Word Part | Meaning |
|-----------|---------|-----------|---------|
| ambi-, amphi- | both | doc(t)- | to teach |
| flam- | fire | medi- | middle |
| simil-, simul- | same, like | mne- | to remember |
| anim- | life, spirit | flor- | flower |
| nat- | to be born | err- | to wander |

## Matching

_____ 1. amnesia

_____ 2. amphibian

_____ 3. doctrine

_____ 4. erratic

_____ 5. facsimile

_____ 6. flamboyant

_____ 7. Florida

_____ 8. mediterranean

_____ 9. nationality

_____ 10. unanimous

A. partial or total loss of memory

B. U.S. state named after Spanish word for "flowery"

C. highly elaborate; having wavy lines and flame-like form

D. many in complete agreement

E. an animal capable of living both on land and in water

F. a principle or system taught for acceptance and belief

G. surrounded nearly or completely by dry land; in the middle of land

H. having no fixed or regular course; wandering

I. the state of belonging to a particular nation by birth

J. an exact copy, reproduction of something

## Definitions

**Directions:** Define the words below.

1. ambidextrous _____

_____

2. medieval _____

_____

3. magnanimous _____

_____

4. neonatal _____

_____

5. florist _____

_____

# Unit 19 (cont.)

## Affix Practice

**Directions:** Fill in the blanks as directed. Use previous worksheets as examples, if needed.

**Word:** _____ dissimilar _____

**Root Element:** _____ simil _____    **Meaning:** _____ same, like _____

**Affix Element:** _____    **Meaning:** _____

| Verb | Adjective | Adverb | Noun |
|------|-----------|--------|------|
|      |           |        |      |

## Extended Activity

Both *inflammable* and *flammable* mean the same thing: easily ignited and capable of burning rapidly. These words are confusing because typically the prefix *in* negates a word. So many people assume that *inflammable* is the opposite of *flammable*.

➤ What word would be the opposite of *inflammable* and *flammable*?

_____

➤ Can you think of any other words whose meanings don't change much when you add an affix? List a few.

_____

_____

_____

_____

# Unit 19 Quiz

## Word Roots

**Directions:** Identify the root and write it on the first line. On the next, tell what the root means. Then define the whole word on the last line.

1. **median**
   Root: _____
   Root Meaning: _____
   Word Definition: _____

2. **documentary**
   Root: _____
   Root Meaning: _____
   Word Definition: _____

3. **amphibious**
   Root: _____
   Root Meaning: _____
   Word Definition: _____

4. **native**
   Root: _____
   Root Meaning: _____
   Word Definition: _____

5. **animation**
   Root: _____
   Root Meaning: _____
   Word Definition: _____

6. **simile**
   Root: _____
   Root Meaning: _____
   Word Definition: _____

7. **flora**
   Root: _____
   Root Meaning: _____
   Word Definition: _____

8. **erroneous**
   Root: _____
   Root Meaning: _____
   Word Definition: _____

9. **amnesiac**
   Root: _____
   Root Meaning: _____
   Word Definition: _____

10. **nonflammable**
    Root: _____
    Root Meaning: _____
    Word Definition: _____

## Matching

**Directions:** Match each word to its definition.

_____ 11. ambiguous      _____ 16. errata

_____ 12. flambeau      _____ 17. national monument

_____ 13. mediocre      _____ 18. florescence

_____ 14. mnemonic      _____ 19. animism

_____ 15. doctrinaire      _____ 20. simultaneous

A. a landmark maintained by a nation's government

B. a state or period of being in bloom

C. errors, mistakes

D. capable of being understood in more than one way; both ways

E. attribution of life to objects

F. a flaming torch

G. ordinary; middle of the road

H. occurring at the same time

I. one who teaches abstract theory without regard to practical difficulties

J. assisting memory

# Unit 20

| Word Part | Meaning |
|---|---|
| cad-, cid- | to fall |
| bell(i)- | war |
| cycl- | circle |
| fal(l)- | to deceive |
| voc- | to call out |

| Word Part | Meaning |
|---|---|
| clud-, claus- | shut, close |
| dia- | across, through |
| scend- | to climb |
| super- | above, beyond |

## Matching

_____ 1. advocate

_____ 2. bellatrix

_____ 3. cyclone

_____ 4. deciduous

_____ 5. descendant

_____ 6. diagonal

_____ 7. falsetto

_____ 8. preclude

_____ 9. supersonic

A. a storm with winds that rotate in a circular motion

B. extending across from one corner to another

C. an artificially high voice

D. one who pleads another's case

E. to make impossible, to prevent, to "shut out"

F. falling off at the end of a period of growth, like leaves

G. proceeding from an ancestor or source, "to climb back"

H. female warrior

I. above the normal speed of sound

## Definitions

**Directions:** Define the words below. The word in italics is fabricated.

10. transcend _____

_____

11. *postbellum* _____

_____

12. claustrophobia _____

_____

13. diameter _____

_____

14. equivocate _____

_____

15. supernumerary _____

_____

# Unit 20 *(cont.)*

## Affix Practice

**Directions:** Fill in the blanks as directed.  Use previous worksheets as examples, if needed.

**Word:** _____ supervision _____

**Root Element:** _____ vis _____          **Meaning:** _____ to see _____

**Affix Element:** _____          **Meaning:** _____

| Verb | Adjective | Adverb | Noun |
|------|-----------|--------|------|
|      |           |        |      |

## Extended Activity

**Extra Word:** Cyclops

**Definition:** any of the mythical giants having one large eye in the center of the forehead

**Directions:** Answer this question:

➤ Can you think of any other real or mythical beings that are named because of their physical features?  Name a few.

_____

_____

_____

_____

# Unit 20 Quiz

## Word Roots

**Directions:** Identify the root and write it on the first line. On the next, tell what the root means. Then define the whole word on the last line.

1. **dial**
   Root: _____
   Root Meaning: _____
   Word Definition: _____

2. **false**
   Root: _____
   Root Meaning: _____
   Word Definition: _____

3. **ascend**
   Root: _____
   Root Meaning: _____
   Word Definition: _____

4. **claustrophobia**
   Root: _____
   Root Meaning: _____
   Word Definition: _____

5. **supervision**
   Root: _____
   Root Meaning: _____
   Word Definition: _____

6. **cyclical**
   Root: _____
   Root Meaning: _____
   Word Definition: _____

7. **cadence**
   Root: _____
   Root Meaning: _____
   Word Definition: _____

8. **include**
   Root: _____
   Root Meaning: _____
   Word Definition: _____

9. **bellicose**
   Root: _____
   Root Meaning: _____
   Word Definition: _____

10. **vocative**
    Root: _____
    Root Meaning: _____
    Word Definition: _____

# Unit 20 Quiz *(cont.)*

## Matching

**Directions:** Match each word to its definition.

_____ 11. belligerent

_____ 12. cyclotron

_____ 13. infallible

_____ 14. seclude

_____ 15. vociferous

_____ 16. deciduate

_____ 17. condescension

_____ 18. supersaturate

_____ 19. diapason

_____ 20. cadaver

A. noisy; (speaking) loudly

B. to cause a chemical solution to be more highly concentrated than is normally possible

C. the manner of dealing with people as if they are below you in class; "climbing down"

D. a circular accelerator

E. hostile; waging war

F. characterized by shedding

G. a dead body, corpse; "fall out of life"

H. incapable of error or making a mistake

I. to shut out from all others; isolate

J. full tonal range; "through all tones"

# Units 17–20 Review

**Directions:** Match the definitions on page 97 to the words below.

_____ 1. amphibious

_____ 2. animosity

_____ 3. ascendancy

_____ 4. chromium

_____ 5. counterclaim

_____ 6. decadence

_____ 7. diathermy

_____ 8. directive

_____ 9. doctorate

_____ 10. dodecagon

_____ 11. egotist

_____ 12. epicenter

_____ 13. errant

_____ 14. exclude

_____ 15. fallacy

_____ 16. flambeau

_____ 17. florid

_____ 18. herbarium

_____ 19. heterosexual

_____ 20. mediate

_____ 21. mnemonic

_____ 22. morphology

_____ 23. motorcycle

_____ 24. orthopedics

_____ 25. pendant

_____ 26. podiatry

_____ 27. postscript

_____ 28. prenatal

_____ 29. provocation

_____ 30. pyrotechnics

_____ 31. rebellion

_____ 32. retroactive

_____ 33. ribosome

_____ 34. simile

_____ 35. subordinate

_____ 36. supersonic

_____ 37. territory

_____ 38. vista

_____ 39. vociferous

_____ 40. voluntary

# Units 17–20 Review *(cont.)*

## Definitions

A. something that directs or impels to a goal or action

B. one's devotion to one's own interests, advancement

C. a bluish-white metallic element used in alloys

D. a display of fireworks taking great skill

E. "crying out in opposition"

F. of or relating to different sexes

G. a hanging ornament

H. any of RNA-rich cytoplasm granules in a body's cell that are sites of protein synthesis

I. the medical treatment and care of feet

J. done, made, or given freely

K. a twelve-sided figure

L. a note added after a letter is completed

M. made effective as of a date prior to enactment

N. to place in a rank or class under, below

O. a distant view through, along an avenue or opening

P. geographical area belonging to or under the jurisdiction of a government authority

Q. medicine dealing with correction or prevention of skeletal deformities

R. the point on Earth's surface directly above an earthquake's point of origin

S. the branch of biology that deals with form and structure of organisms

T. a collection of dried plants

U. living a double life

V. ill will, spirit; resentment

W. a flaming torch

X. likeness, comparison

Y. taking place before birth

Z. the degree, title, or rank of a doctor

AA. to work with opposing sides as a controlling agent; "middle man"

BB. assisting memory

CC. very flowery in style

DD. wandering from an accepted position

EE. deterioration, decline

FF. resistance to authority

GG. two-wheeled automotive vehicle

HH. a false or mistaken idea

II. something that incites anger

JJ. to prevent from using; to shut out

KK. the generation of heat through tissue by electric currents for surgical purposes

LL. controlling influence; domination

MM. relating to speeds one to five times above the normal speed of sound

NN. noisy; (speaking) loudly

# Vocabulary List

**arachnid**

arthropod with four pairs of legs, lung-like sacs or breathing tubes, and body divided into two segments

**cereal**

relating to grain or the plants that produce it

**cerebral**

of the upper, main part of the brain of vertebrate animals

**cloth**

a woven, knitted, or pressed fabric of fibrous material

**echo**

the repeating of a sound, produced by reflection of sound waves from a surface

**electricity**

a form of energy generated by friction, induction, or chemical, and radiant effects

**Herculean**

requiring tremendous strength; strong

**hygiene**

a science concerned with maintaining or establishing good health

**hypnosis**

a sleeplike condition physically induced, usually by another person

**iridescent**

rainbow-like, colorful

**jovial**

jolly, hearty, joyful

**lunatic**

insane, extremely foolish

**mercurial**

changeable; swift

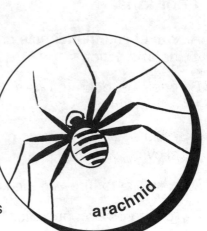

arachnid

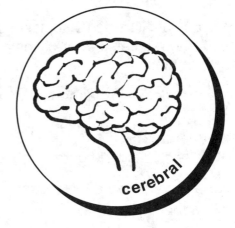

cerebral

Herculean

# Vocabulary List *(cont.)*

**narcissistic**

self-absorbed; exceedingly vain; conceited; in love with oneself

**nemesis**

a deadly adversary; enemy

**panic**

wild, frightful chaos; inexplicable terror

**phoenix**

something that is reborn from its own destruction

**rumor**

an unconfirmed report

**saturnine**

gloomy; taciturn, depressed

**somnambulate**

to walk while asleep; sleepwalking

**stentorian**

extremely loud

**tantalize**

to torment or tease with unattainable things

**thespian**

relating to drama; actor, actress

**titanic**

powerful, huge, colossal, massive

**volcano**

a vent in Earth's crust through which rocks, dust, ash, or molten rock in the form of liquid magma is ejected

# Unit 21

## Matching

_____ 1. Monday

_____ 2. Tuesday

_____ 3. Wednesday

_____ 4. Thursday

_____ 5. Friday

_____ 6. Saturday

_____ 7. Sunday

A. the Sun's day

B. day named after Woden, chief Germanic god

C. day named after Tiw, Germanic god of war and sky

D. day named after Saturn, ancient Roman god

E. the moon's day

F. day named after Thor, Germanic god of thunder

G. day named after Freija, Germanic goddess of life and beauty

## Definitions

**Directions:** Define the words below. Use a dictionary, if necessary. Then tell the origins of the words.

8. mercurial_____

9. Herculean _____

10. saturnine_____

11. nemesis _____

12. jovial _____

13. tantalize _____

14. titanic _____

15. narcissistic _____

## Extended Activity

**Extra Word:** procrustean

**Definition:** designed to secure conformity at any cost

**Directions:** This word comes from *Procrustes*, who was a cruel innkeeper. He told his customers that everyone fits the beds in the inn. What he didn't tell them is *how* they would fit. If a customer was too short, Procrustes would stretch them until they fit. If a customer was too tall, he would cut off their feet and legs so they'd fit.

Can you think of another word—one that's not on any of your worksheets—that is named after a famous or mythological person and the actions he or she is known for? Write it below and give its definition.

➤ Word: _____

➤ Definition: _____

# Unit 22

## Matching

_____ 1. January

_____ 2. February

_____ 3. March

_____ 4. April

_____ 5. May

_____ 6. June

_____ 7. July

_____ 8. August

_____ 9. September

_____ 10. October

_____ 11. November

_____ 12. December

A. named after Juno, wife of Jupiter

B. names after Janus, two-faced Roman god of beginnings

C. tenth month

D. ninth month

E. named after Freija, Germanic goddess of love

F. seventh month

G. named after Maia, Roman goddess of life and beauty

H. named after Mars, Roman god of war

I. eighth month

J. named after Julius Caesar

K. named after Aphrodite, Greek goddess of love

L. named after Augustus Caesar

## Definitions

**Directions:** Define the words below.

13. hypnosis _____

14. panic _____

15. iridescent _____

16. lunatic _____

17. stentorian _____

## Extended Activity

**Extra Word:** Circean

**Definition:** dangerously bewitching

**Directions:** This word comes from Circe, a sorceress with whom Odysseus spent a lot of time. It's another example of a word based on the actions of a mythological figure. Can you make up a word based on a famous or mythological person and the things he or she is known for? Give it a try.

➤ Word: _____

➤ Definition: _____

_____

# Unit 23

## Matching

_____ 1. Aquarius

_____ 2. Aries

_____ 3. Cancer

_____ 4. Capricorn

_____ 5. Gemini

_____ 6. Leo

_____ 7. Libra

_____ 8. Pisces

_____ 9. Sagittarius

_____ 10. Scorpio

_____ 11. Taurus

_____ 12. Virgo

A. 3rd sign of zodiac; Latin root meaning "twin"

B. 1st sign of zodiac; represented by the ram

C. 2nd sign of zodiac; represented by the bull

D. 12th sign of zodiac; Latin root meaning "fish"

E. 4th sign of zodiac; constellation in the Northern Hemisphere

F. 10th sign of zodiac; Latin root meaning "goat-horned"

G. 8th sign of zodiac; Latin root meaning "scorpion"

H. constellation in celestial equator; Latin root meaning "virgin"

I. 9th sign of zodiac; named for an archer

J. 5th sign of zodiac; Latin root meaning "lion"

K. 7th sign of zodiac; Latin for "balance"

L. the 11th sign of the zodiac; its root means "water"

## Definitions

**Directions:** Define the words below.

13. somnambulate _____

14. cloth _____

15. hygiene _____

16. cereal _____

17. thespian _____

## Extended Activity

**Directions:** Answer these questions:

➢ What sign of the Zodiac are you? _____

➢ What are some personality traits that people born under your Zodiac sign are supposed to have? (You may need to do research to find this information.) _____

_____

➢ Do you feel you fit the description of the traits you've just listed? Why or why not?

_____

_____

# Unit 24

## Matching

_____ 1. Mercury

_____ 2. Venus

_____ 3. Earth

_____ 4. Mars

_____ 5. Jupiter

_____ 6. Saturn

_____ 7. Uranus

_____ 8. Neptune

_____ 9. Pluto

A. the third largest planet; from Poseidon

B. the planet whose revolution around the sun is 365 days and whose axial rotation is nearly 24 hours; from Gaea

C. the smallest and [usually] outermost planet in the solar system; from Hades

D. the second largest planet in the solar system; from Cronus

E. the planet seventh in distance from the sun; from father of the Titans

F. the most brilliant planet in the solar system; from Aphrodite

G. the planet that is red in color; from the god of war

H. the largest planet; from the king of the gods

I. the planet that is closest to the sun and fastest moving

## Definitions

**Directions:** Define the words below.

10. rumor _____

11. electricity _____

12. volcano _____

13. phoenix _____

14. cerebral _____

15. arachnid _____

16. echo _____

## Extended Activity

**Directions:** Achilles was the Greek hero of the Trojan War who was killed by an arrow at his heel. The expression "Achilles heel" means a weakness. Do research to find out why Achilles' heel was vulnerable. Write a short paragraph about it.

_____

_____

_____

_____

# Units 21–24 Quiz

## Matching, Part I

**Directions:** Match each word to its definition.

_____ 1. mercurial

_____ 2. iridescent

_____ 3. hypnosis

_____ 4. volcano

_____ 5. echo

_____ 6. phoenix

_____ 7. arachnid

_____ 8. jovial

_____ 9. cereal

_____ 10. nemesis

A. relating to grain or the plants that produce it

B. rainbow-like, colorful

C. the repeating of a sound, produced by reflection of sound waves from a surface

D. jolly, hearty, joyful

E. a vent in Earth's crust through which rocks, dust, ash, or molten rock in the form of liquid magma is ejected

F. changeable; swift

G. a deadly adversary, enemy

H. a sleeplike condition physically induced, usually by another person

I. something that is reborn from its own destruction

J. arthropod with four pairs of legs, lung-like sacs or breathing tubes, and body divided into two segments

## Matching, Part II

**Directions:** Match each word to its definition.

_____ 11. cerebral

_____ 12. titanic

_____ 13. stentorian

_____ 14. cloth

_____ 15. lunatic

_____ 16. Herculean

_____ 17. saturnine

_____ 18. narcissistic

_____ 19. hygiene

_____ 20. panic

_____ 21. thespian

_____ 22. rumor

_____ 23. somnambulate

_____ 24. electricity

_____ 25. tantalize

K. requiring tremendous strength; strong

L. an unconfirmed report

M. gloomy; taciturn, depressed

N. powerful, huge, colossal, massive

O. to walk while asleep; sleepwalking

P. a form of energy generated by friction, induction, or chemical, and radiant effects

Q. relating to drama; actor, actress

R. insane

S. of the upper, main part of the brain of vertebrate animals

T. self-absorbed; exceedingly vain; conceited; in love with oneself

U. extremely loud

V. wild, frightful chaos; inexplicable terror

W. to torment or tease with unattainable things

X. a woven, knitted, or pressed fabric of fibrous material

Y. a study concerned with maintaining or establishing good health

# Vocabulary List

| Word Part | Meaning |
|-----------|---------|
| act | to do, act, drive |
| acro | topmost, high |
| agon | struggle |
| ambu | to go, to walk |
| angel | messenger |
| counter, contr | against, opposite |
| dyna | power |
| endo | in, into, within |
| erg | work |
| exo | out of, outside |
| fen | to ward, strike off |
| fix | to fasten |
| flect, flex | to bend, twist |
| holo | whole |
| inter | between |
| intra, intro | within |
| magn | large |
| mania | madness |
| min | small |
| misc, mix | to mix |
| mor(t) | death |
| mot | to move |

# Vocabulary List *(cont.)*

| Word Part | Meaning |
|---|---|
| necro | corpse |
| noct | night |
| nov | new |
| ord | order |
| pan | all |
| par | to give birth to |
| para | alongside |
| pli(c), ply | fold, bend |
| pre | before |
| proto | first |
| pun(c) | to stab, point |
| rex, reg | king |
| rupt | to break |
| sci | to know |
| sign | a mark, seal, sign |
| solv, solut | free, loosen |
| son | hearing, sound |
| the(s) | to put, place |
| type | a blow, impression |
| xeno | strange, foreign |

# Unit 25

| Word Part | Meaning | Word Part | Meaning |
|---|---|---|---|
| act- | to do, to act, drive | acro- | topmost, high |
| erg- | work | inter- | between |
| rex-, reg- | king | necro- | corpse |
| par- | to give birth to | fix- | to fasten |
| sci- | to know | rupt- | to break |

## Matching

_____ 1. acrobat

_____ 2. bankrupt

_____ 3. ergomaniac

_____ 4. interject

_____ 5. interrex

_____ 6. necropolis

_____ 7. parenthood

_____ 8. prefix

_____ 9. subconscious

_____ 10. transaction

A. knowledge existing in the mind without awareness

B. performer of gymnastic feats

C. king between successive kings; a temporary king

D. a business deal; the act of carrying out business

E. reduced to financial ruin

F. to place before; to "fasten" to the beginning of a word

G. a workaholic

H. to throw between or among other things

I. the act of caring for and bringing up others

J. cemetery; "a city of the dead"

## Definitions

**Directions:** Define the words below.

1. postpartum _____

_____

2. acrophobia _____

_____

3. regicide _____

_____

4. omniscient _____

_____

5. interaction _____

_____

# Unit 25 *(cont.)*

## Affix Practice

**Directions:** Fill in the blanks as directed.  Use previous worksheets for example, if needed.

**Word:** _____ disrupt _____

**Root Element:** _____ rupt _____    **Meaning:** _____ to break _____

**Affix Element:** _____    **Meaning:** _____

| Verb | Adjective | Adverb | Noun |
|------|-----------|--------|------|
|      |           |        |      |

## Extended Activity

**Extra Word:** acronym

**Definition:** a word formed from the initial letter(s) of each of the successive parts or major parts of a compound term

**Directions:** Some well-known acronyms would include NASA (National Aeronautics and Space Administration) and radar (radio detecting and ranging).  Can you think of any others? List three and show what each letter in the acronym stands for.

| Acronym | Stands For |
|---------|-----------|
|         |           |

# Unit 25 Quiz

## Word Roots

**Directions:** Identify the root and write it on the first line. On the next, tell what the root means. Then define the whole word on the last line.

1. **intercept**
   Root: _____
   Root Meaning: _____
   Word Definition: _____

2. **scientist**
   Root: _____
   Root Meaning: _____
   Word Definition: _____

3. **suffix**
   Root: _____
   Root Meaning: _____
   Word Definition: _____

4. **necrosis**
   Root: _____
   Root Meaning: _____
   Word Definition: _____

5. **ergonomic**
   Root: _____
   Root Meaning: _____
   Word Definition: _____

6. **tyrannosaurus rex**
   Root: _____
   Root Meaning: _____
   Word Definition: _____

7. **acrophobia**
   Root: _____
   Root Meaning: _____
   Word Definition: _____

8. **parentage**
   Root: _____
   Root Meaning: _____
   Word Definition: _____

9. **corrupt**
   Root: _____
   Root Meaning: _____
   Word Definition: _____

10. **regimen**
    Root: _____
    Root Meaning: _____
    Word Definition: _____

## Matching

**Directions:** Match each word to its definition.

_____ 11. conscience

_____ 12. acropolis

_____ 13. fixation

_____ 14. necromancy

_____ 15. regent

_____ 16. interrex

_____ 17. rupture

_____ 18. reactive

_____ 19. parental

_____ 20. ergophobia

A. tending to be responsive to a stimulus; acting to a stimulus

B. knowing the difference between right and wrong

C. one acting as a ruler

D. a breaking open or bursting

E. fatherly or motherly

F. fortified height of ancient Greek city

G. a strong attachment to a person, thing

H. a fear of work or working

I. the art of conjuring up and communing with the spirits of the dead in order to predict the future

J. king between successive kings; a temporary king

# Unit 26 Words

| Word Part | Meaning | Word Part | Meaning |
|---|---|---|---|
| angel- | messenger | son- | hearing, sound |
| dyna- | power | exo-, ecto- | out of, outside |
| endo- | in, into, within | the(s)- | to put, place |
| holo- | whole | pan- | all |
| agon- | struggle | proto- | first |

## Matching

_____ 1. Angeleno

_____ 2. consonant

_____ 3. dynasty

_____ 4. ectogenous

_____ 5. endothermic

_____ 6. epithet

_____ 7. holograph

_____ 8. panchromatic

_____ 9. protagonist

_____ 10. protozoan

A. caused or produced by factors outside the organism

B. a document wholly handwritten by the author

C. a native or inhabitant of Los Angeles ("the city of angels")

D. having harmony or agreement in sound; not *a*, *e*, *i*, *o*, or *u*

E. any of a phylum or subkingdom of unicellular lower invertebrate animals; "first animals"

F. a term used as a descriptive substitute for a person's name or title

G. a succession of rulers from the same family; a powerful family or group

H. sensitive to all colors of visible light

I. a principal character in a story; the leader or supporter of a cause

J. characterized by or formed by the absorption of heat

# Unit 26 *(cont.)*

## Matching

**Directions:** Define the words below. The words in italics are fabricated.

1. antagonist _____

   _____

2. thermodynamics _____

   _____

3. unison _____

   _____

4. synthesize _____

   _____

5. pantheism _____

   _____

6. *hologynic* _____

   _____

7. *protolithic* _____

   _____

8. endocardium _____

   _____

9. exobiology _____

   _____

10. archangel _____

   _____

## Extended Activity

**Extra Word:** evangelist

**Definition:** a preacher who travels from revival to revival spreading his or her message

**Directions:** Answer these questions:

➤ What is a *televangelist*? _____

➤ Can you think of any other words that have been changed or created because of new technology? Name two words and give their definitions.

| Word | Definition |
|------|------------|
|      |            |
|      |            |

# Unit 26 Quiz

## Word Roots

**Directions:** Identify the root and write it on the first line. On the next line, tell what the root means. Then define the whole word on the last line.

1. **evangelical**
   Root: _____
   Root Meaning: _____
   Word Definition: _____

2. **agony**
   Root: _____
   Root Meaning: _____
   Word Definition: _____

3. **epithet**
   Root: _____
   Root Meaning: _____
   Word Definition: _____

4. **exotic**
   Root: _____
   Root Meaning: _____
   Word Definition: _____

5. **sonic boom**
   Root: _____
   Root Meaning: _____
   Word Definition: _____

6. **protolithic**
   Root: _____
   Root Meaning: _____
   Word Definition: _____

7. **dynamite**
   Root: _____
   Root Meaning: _____
   Word Definition: _____

8. **Holocene**
   Root: _____
   Root Meaning: _____
   Word Definition: _____

9. **pantomime**
   Root: _____
   Root Meaning: _____
   Word Definition: _____

10. **endocrine**
    Root: _____
    Root Meaning: _____
    Word Definition: _____

# Unit 26 Quiz *(cont.)*

## Matching

**Directions:** Match the words to their definitions.

_____ 11. hydrodynamics      _____ 16. protocol

_____ 12. dissonant        _____ 17. holocaust

_____ 13. endometrium       _____ 18. exogeneous

_____ 14. thesis         _____ 19. antagonist

_____ 15. Pan-American      _____ 20. archangel

---

A. one who opposes a principal character

B. jarring, harsh, clashing

C. great or total destruction by fire; burnt whole

D. of or pertaining to North, South, and Central America collectively

E. a celestial being next in rank above angel

F. the power of fluids in motion

G. a proposition to be maintained or proven

H. caused or produced by factors outside the organism

I. official formality

J. the mucous membrane lining the uterus

# Unit 27

| Word Part | Meaning | Word Part | Meaning |
|---|---|---|---|
| ord- | order | pun(c)- | to stab, point |
| misc-, mix- | to mix | mania- | madness |
| noct- | night | nov- | new |
| fen- | to ward, strike off | sign- | a mark, sign, seal |
| type- | a blow, impression | xeno- | strange, foreign |

## Matching

_____ 1. disorder

_____ 2. miscellaneous

_____ 3. nocturnal

_____ 4. offense

_____ 5. prototype

_____ 6. puncture

_____ 7. pyromania

_____ 8. renovation

_____ 9. signature

_____ 10. xenophobe

A. to pierce or poke a hole in something

B. lack of order; disturbance

C. a person afraid of foreigners

D. the name of a person as written by himself; a sign used to indicate key or tempo

E. restoration to an earlier condition

F. the uncontrollable impulse to start fires

G. made up of a variety of parts, members, or characteristics

H. a crime; the act of attacking or assaulting

I. an original model or form

J. of, relating to, occurring in the night

## Definitions

**Directions:** Define the words below. The words in italics are fabricated.

1. typescript _____

_____

2. equinoctial _____

_____

3. *mixologist* _____

_____

4. *xenophile* _____

_____

5. novice _____

_____

# Unit 27 *(cont.)*

## Affix Practice

**Directions:** Fill in the blanks as directed.  Use previous worksheets for example, if needed.

**Word:** _____ defendant _____

**Root Element:** _____ fen _____        **Meaning:** _to ward, strike off_

**Affix Element:** _____        **Meaning:** _____

| Verb | Adjective | Adverb | Noun |
|------|-----------|--------|------|
|      |           |        |      |

## Extended Activity

**Extra Word:** punctuation

**Definition:** the marks in writing and printing used to separate units and clarify meaning; the marks so used

**Directions:** Rewrite the following sentences, using correct punctuation.

1. Wow  I can't believe my luck_____

   _____

2. Since school ends on May 30th my parents planned our summer vacation for the second week of June _____

   _____

3. Is Janie coming with us asked Samantha _____

   _____

4. My chores include the following  washing and putting away dishes dusting and sweeping my bedroom and taking out the garbage _____

   _____

5. Planes Trains and Automobiles is my favorite movie of all time and It Might Be You is my favorite song. _____

   _____

# Unit 27 Quiz

## Word Roots

**Directions:** Identify the root and write it on the first line. On the next, tell what the root means. Then define the whole word on the last line.

1. **kleptomania**
   Root: _____
   Root Meaning: _____
   Word Definition: _____

2. **extraordinary**
   Root: _____
   Root Meaning: _____
   Word Definition: _____

3. **xenophilia**
   Root: _____
   Root Meaning: _____
   Word Definition: _____

4. **nocturne**
   Root: _____
   Root Meaning: _____
   Word Definition: _____

5. **typify**
   Root: _____
   Root Meaning: _____
   Word Definition: _____

6. **mixed-media**
   Root: _____
   Root Meaning: _____
   Word Definition: _____

7. **novelty**
   Root: _____
   Root Meaning: _____
   Word Definition: _____

8. **compunctions**
   Root: _____
   Root Meaning: _____
   Word Definition: _____

9. **offensive**
   Root: _____
   Root Meaning: _____
   Word Definition: _____

10. **designate**
    Root: _____
    Root Meaning: _____
    Word Definition: _____

# Unit 27 Quiz (cont.)

## Matching

**Directions:** Match the words to their definitions.

_____ 11. noctilucent          _____ 16. xenon

_____ 12. innovation           _____ 17. signatory

_____ 13. megalomaniac         _____ 18. puncheon

_____ 14. miscegenation        _____ 19. typography

_____ 15. coordinate           _____ 20. fencing

A. someone who believes he's larger than he is; obsessed by grand delusions

B. a chemical element named because of its strange composition

C. a person or party who signs a document

D. "night shine"

E. the composition of printed material from movable type

F. introduction of something new

G. the art or sport of swordplay

H. marriage between persons of different races; "mixing races"

I. to bring order to; classify, arrange

J. heavy timber used for stamping in structural framing

# Unit 28

| Word Part | Meaning | | Word Part | Meaning |
|---|---|---|---|---|
| ambu- | to go, to walk | | counter-, contra- | against, opposite |
| flect-, flex- | to bend, twist | | intra-intro- | within |
| magn- | large, great | | min- | small |
| mort(t)- | death | | mot- | to move |
| para- | alongside | | pli(c)-, ply- | to fold, bend |
| pre- | before | | solv-, solut- | free, loosen |

## Matching

_____ 1. ambulance

_____ 2. counterintelligence

_____ 3. flexible

_____ 4. intramural

_____ 5. minimum

_____ 6. mortician

_____ 7. motion

_____ 8. parentheses

_____ 9. prediction

_____ 10. solution

A. the branch of services charged with keeping information from an enemy and preventing sabotage

B. capable of responding to change; able to be bent or twisted

C. a vehicle equipped to transport the sick or wounded

D. the least possible quantity or degree

E. existing within the bounds of an institution, especially a school

F. a funeral director; undertaker

G. the significant movement of a part of the body

H. the answer or disposition to a problem

I. the foretelling of something; a prophecy

J. the upright curved lines used alongside explanatory or qualifying remarks

## Definitions

**Directions:** Define the words below.

11. contradict _____

_____

12. introduce _____

_____

13. magnanimous _____

_____

14. multiplication _____

_____

15. parallel _____

_____

# Unit 28 *(cont.)*

## Affix Practice

**Directions:** Fill in the blanks as directed.  Use previous worksheets as examples, if needed.

**Word:** _____reflect_____

**Root Element:** _____flect_____   **Meaning:** _____to bend, twist_____

**Affix Element:** _____   **Meaning:** _____

| Verb | Adjective | Adverb | Noun |
|------|-----------|--------|------|
|      |           |        |      |

## Extended Activity

**Extra Words:**  magna cum laude

**Definition:**  the second highest honor a graduate student can receive upon graduating

**Directions:**  Do research to find the answer to this question:

➢ What is the graduating honor one step above magna cum laude?

_____

_____

# Unit 28 Quiz

## Word Roots

**Directions:** Identify the root and write it on the first line. On the next, tell what the root means. Then define the whole word on the last line.

1. **comply**
   Root: _____
   Root Meaning: _____
   Word Definition: _____

2. **motive**
   Root: _____
   Root Meaning: _____
   Word Definition: _____

3. **paralegal**
   Root: _____
   Root Meaning: _____
   Word Definition: _____

4. **genuflect**
   Root: _____
   Root Meaning: _____
   Word Definition: _____

5. **minute**
   Root: _____
   Root Meaning: _____
   Word Definition: _____

6. **contraband**
   Root: _____
   Root Meaning: _____
   Word Definition: _____

7. **ambulatory**
   Root: _____
   Root Meaning: _____
   Word Definition: _____

8. **mortgage**
   Root: _____
   Root Meaning: _____
   Word Definition: _____

9. **irresolute**
   Root: _____
   Root Meaning: _____
   Word Definition: _____

10. **presentiment**
    Root: _____
    Root Meaning: _____
    Word Definition: _____

# Unit 28 Quiz (cont.)

## Matching

**Directions:** Match the words to their definitions.

_____ 11. commotion

_____ 12. paraphrase

_____ 13. postmortem

_____ 14. magniloquent

_____ 15. insolvent

_____ 16. presides

_____ 17. triplicate

_____ 18. flexible

_____ 19. countermand

_____ 20. preamble

_____ 21. introvert

_____ 22. minuscule

A. a typed letter that makes three copies; "three folds"

B. very small

C. a person whose thoughts and feelings are directed inward

D. loud or confusing noise

E. free of money; penniless, bankrupt

F. speaking large or in a grand manner

G. an introduction to a formal document; "walking in front"

H. able to bend; able to adapt

I. order against another order

J. "sits before"

K. "after death"

L. "to say alongside," saying the quotation in your own words

# Units 25–28 Review

**Directions:** Match the definitions on page 125 to the words below.

| | | | |
|---|---|---|---|
| _____ | 1. acropolis | _____ | 21. hydrodynamics |
| _____ | 2. preamble | _____ | 22. noctilucent |
| _____ | 3. fixation | _____ | 23. countermand |
| _____ | 4. ambulance | _____ | 24. intramural |
| _____ | 5. minimum | _____ | 25. paraphrase |
| _____ | 6. mortician | _____ | 26. magniloquent |
| _____ | 7. commotion | _____ | 27. insolvent |
| _____ | 8. postmortem | _____ | 28. dissonant |
| _____ | 9. antagonist | _____ | 29. prediction |
| _____ | 10. thesis | _____ | 30. solution |
| _____ | 11. signatory | _____ | 31. motion |
| _____ | 12. innovation | _____ | 32. counterintelligence |
| _____ | 13. megalomaniac | _____ | 33. rupture |
| _____ | 14. xenon | _____ | 34. flexible |
| _____ | 15. coordinate | _____ | 35. minuscule |
| _____ | 16. archangel | _____ | 36. xenophobe |
| _____ | 17. holocaust | _____ | 37. renovation |
| _____ | 18. exogeneous | _____ | 38. prototype |
| _____ | 19. typography | _____ | 39. signature |
| _____ | 20. fencing | _____ | 40. nocturnal |

# Units 25–28 Review *(cont.)*

## Definitions

A. able to bend; able to adapt

B. very small

C. a breaking open or bursting

D. fortified height of ancient Greek city

E. free of money; penniless, bankrupt

F. the significant movement of a part of the body

G. jarring, harsh, clashing

H. one who opposes a principal character

I. great or total destruction by fire; burnt whole

J. someone who believes he's larger than he is; obsessed by grand delusions

K. the name of a person as written by himself; a sign used to indicate key or tempo

L. of, relating to, occurring in the night

M. a person or party who signs a document

N. an original model or form

O. a chemical element named because of its strange composition

P. existing within the bounds of an institution, especially a school

Q. caused or produced by factors outside the organism

R. the power of fluids in motion

S. "night shine"

T. the composition of printed material from movable type

U. the art or sport of swordplay

V. a proposition or dissertation resulting from research that is put in writing

W. a violent agitation, movement

X. the foretelling of something; a prophecy

Y. an introduction to a formal document; "walking in front"

Z. a strong attachment to a person, thing

AA. the answer or disposition to a problem

BB. a funeral director; undertaker

CC. a vehicle equipped to transport the sick or wounded

DD. the least possible quantity or degree

EE. order against another order

FF. "after death"

GG. speaking large or in a grand manner

HH. "to say alongside," saying the quotation in your own words

II. the branch of services charged with keeping information from an enemy and preventing sabotage

JJ. a person afraid of foreigners

KK. introduction of something new

LL. to bring order to; classify, arrange

MM. restoration to an earlier condition

NN. a celestial being next in rank above angel

# Unit 29

## Which One Doesn't Belong?

**Directions:** The following groups of words have something in common except for one word. Circle the word that doesn't belong.

**Example:** circumference    perimeter    (kilogram)

**Explanation:** The word *kilogram* would be circled because the first two words include the roots *circum* and *peri*, which mean "around." They also refer to the distance around something. *Kilogram* refers to the weight of something.

| | | | |
|---|---|---|---|
| 1. misanthrope | gynecologist | virile | androgen |
| 2. monarch | democracy | pedagogue | automaton |
| 3. subscription | inspection | biography | prescribe |
| 4. moronic | bibliophile | recognize | autonomy |
| 5. cardiologist | osteopathy | epidermis | lithography |

## True or False

**Directions:** Write **T** on the line next to **true** statements. Write **F** on the line next to **false** statements. Correct each false statement and rewrite it.

_____ 6. *Theology* is the writing of gods. _____

_____

_____ 7. An *omnivore* is a meat-eating animal. _____

_____

_____ 8. Someone who has *acrophobia* is afraid of heights. _____

_____

_____ 9. A *millipede* is an insect with a million legs. _____

_____

_____ 10. The word *geocentric* refers to Earth being the center of the universe. _____

_____

_____

## Combining Roots

**Directions:** Combine the following roots and write the word on the line. Then tell the meaning of the word.

11. **pseudo + pod =**

    Word: _____

    Definition: _____

12. **phobo + phobia =**

    Word: _____

    Definition: _____

13. **penta + gon =**

    Word: _____

    Definition: _____

14. **aqua + polis =**

    Word: _____

    Definition: _____

15. **icthyo + logy =**

    Word: _____

    Definition: _____

## Word Tree

**Directions:** Complete a word tree using the word *synchronize*.

**Word 1:** synchronize

**Definition:** _____

_____

**Word 2A:** _____

**Definition:** _____

_____

**Word 2B:** _____

**Definition:** _____

_____

**Word 3A:** _____

**Definition:** _____

_____

**Word 3B:** _____

**Definition:** _____

_____

**Word 3C:** _____

**Definition:** _____

_____

# Unit 30 Words

## Matching

| | | | |
|---|---|---|---|
| _____ | 1. philanthropy | A. | measures the intensity of sound |
| _____ | 2. hypothermia | B. | universe where the sun is the center |
| _____ | 3. euphony | C. | three-legged stand |
| _____ | 4. tripod | D. | of the same color |
| _____ | 5. psychosomatic | E. | condition of reduced temperature |
| _____ | 6. xenophobia | F. | love of mankind |
| _____ | 7. sympathy | G. | pleasant sounding |
| _____ | 8. phonometer | H. | physical disorder due to mental state |
| _____ | 9. heliocentric | I. | feeling that is the same as another |
| _____ | 10. homochromous | J. | fear of strangers |

## Which One Doesn't Belong?

**Directions:** The following groups of words have something in common except for one word. Circle the word that doesn't belong. Refer to page 126 for an example, if needed.

| | | | |
|---|---|---|---|
| 11. dermatitis | ophthalmology | osteopathy | meteorology |
| 12. polygyny | quadruplets | demigod | century |
| 13. telephone | auditorium | sonar | spectator |
| 14. sororicide | tetrahedron | patriarch | maternal |
| 15. marine | transport | nausea | hydrophobia |

# Unit 30 (cont.)

## True or False

**Directions:** Write **T** on the line next to **true** statements. Write **F** on the line next to **false** statements. Correct each false statement.

_____ 16. *November* is the eleventh month in the Roman calendar.

_____ 17. *Polytheism* is the belief in many gods.

_____ 18. A *microscope* can be used to measure small distances.

_____ 19. A small world or universe would be called a *macrocosm*.

_____ 20. *Geology* is the study of Earth.

## Word Tree

**Directions:** Use the words provided to complete the word trees below.

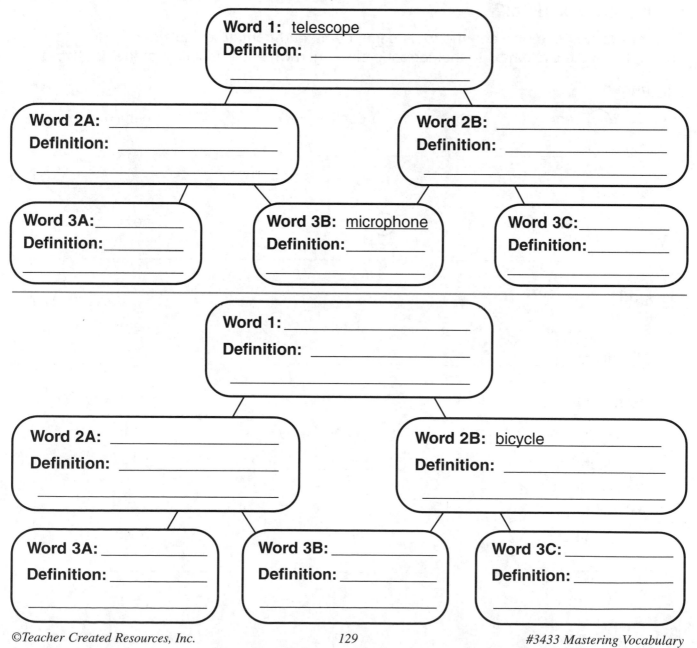

**Word 1:** telescope
**Definition:** _____

**Word 2A:** _____
**Definition:** _____

**Word 2B:** _____
**Definition:** _____

**Word 3A:** _____
**Definition:** _____

**Word 3B:** microphone
**Definition:** _____

**Word 3C:** _____
**Definition:** _____

**Word 1:** _____
**Definition:** _____

**Word 2A:** _____
**Definition:** _____

**Word 2B:** bicycle
**Definition:** _____

**Word 3A:** _____
**Definition:** _____

**Word 3B:** _____
**Definition:** _____

**Word 3C:** _____
**Definition:** _____

# Unit 31

## True or False

**Directions:** Write **T** on the line next to **true** statements. Write **F** on the line next to **false** statements. Correct each false statement.

_____ 1. A *cryptogram* would be something written in secret.

_____ 2. *Photograph* technically means "written picture."

_____ 3. Someone with *dual* personalities has several different ones.

_____ 4. A *sophomore* technically means "a wise fool."

_____ 5. A *valediction* is a farewell speech.

## Semi, Demi, or Hemi?

**Directions:** Choose between the roots **semi**, **demi**, and **hemi** to complete the following words. Fill in the circle next to the correct prefix. Then write the definition of the new word.

6. **annual**

    ○ semi          ○ demi          ○ hemi

    Definition: _____

7. **sphere**

    ○ semi          ○ demi          ○ hemi

    Definition: _____

8. **god**

    ○ semi          ○ demi          ○ hemi

    Definition: _____

9. **permeable**

    ○ semi          ○ demi          ○ hemi

    Definition: _____

10. **weekly**

    ○ semi          ○ demi          ○ hemi

    Definition: _____

# Unit 31 (cont.)

## Fill in the Circle

**Directions:** In each of the following, fill in the circle next to the word containing the root element of the capitalized word(s).

**Example:** NEW

    (a) noxious    (b) microbe    (c) monologue    **(d) novice**

**Explanation:** Letter d is what you would choose because *nov* means "new."

11. TO BRING, CARRY

    (a) superfluous    (b) transport    (c) contradiction    (d) vision

12. STRAIGHT

    (a) omniscient    (b) amorous    (c) correction    (d) politician

13. SOUND

    (a) hydraulics    (b) Paleolithic    (c) loquacious    (d) telephone

14. FEELINGS

    (a) apathetic    (b) symmetry    (c) inaudible    (d) mission

15. TO ASK, SEEK

    (a) inspiring    (b) verbose    (c) progress    (d) inquisitive

16. COLD

    (a) mesoderm    (b) temporal    (c) cryogenics    (d) digress

17. INSECTS

    (a) entomology    (b) etymology    (c) numerology    (d) ornithology

18. EARTH

    (a) nautical    (b) terrarium    (c) flamboyant    (d) aquatic

19. BOTH

    (a) prototype    (b) ambivalence    (c) antagonistic    (d) flexible

20. TO SEND

    (a) transmission    (b) voracity    (c) infidel    (d) concession

## Which One Doesn't Belong?

**Directions:** The following words all have something in common except for one. Circle the one that doesn't belong.

| | | | |
|---|---|---|---|
| 21. misanthrope | malicious | arachnophobia | retrograde |
| 22. regicide | bilingual | hexameter | unilateral |
| 23. astronomy | soliloquy | solstice | lunacy |
| 24. hypertension | megalopolis | microcosm | magnificent |
| 25. tautology | homogenous | simultaneous | xenocentric |

# Unit 32

## Matching

**Directions:** Match each word to its definition. Use previous worksheets if the words can't be found in a dictionary.

_____ 1. antisymmetric

_____ 2. astronaut

_____ 3. bibliomania

_____ 4. genocide

_____ 5. macroscopic

_____ 6. monocentric

_____ 7. perihelion

_____ 8. psychonomic

_____ 9. telethermometer

_____ 10. triarchy

A. killing of a race

B. centered around one

C. apparatus that indicates temperature of a distant point

D. visible to the naked eye

E. government or rule by three persons

F. having opposite, irregular properties

G. that point in a planet's orbit path that is closest to the sun around which it travels

H. obsession with books

I. knowledge of the mind

J. literally, "star traveler"

## Numerical Order

**Directions:** Arrange the words in order based on the numerical value of the root. Arrange them with "A" being the first word and continue through the alphabet.

_____ 11. octagon

_____ 12. tetrameter

_____ 13. duet

_____ 14. semicircle

_____ 15. centigrade

_____ 16. December

_____ 17. Pentateuch

_____ 18. milliliter

_____ 19. quarterly

_____ 20. sextuplets

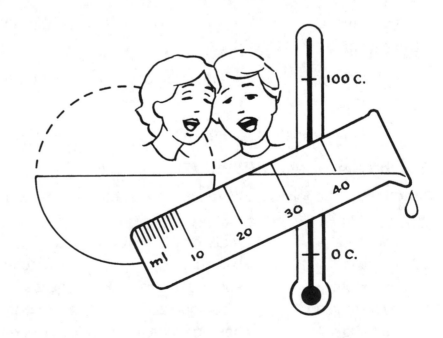

## Matching

**Directions:** Match the root on the left with the root on the right that means the same thing.

_____ 21. pyr                    A. meso

_____ 22. circum                 B. sens, sent

_____ 23. philo                  C. amor

_____ 24. scop                   D. multi

_____ 25. syn, sym               E. flam

_____ 26. poly                   F. peri

_____ 27. bene                   G. loqu

_____ 28. dict                   H. vid, vis

_____ 29. path                   I. simil, simul

_____ 30. medi                   J. eu

## Matching

**Directions:** Match the root on the left with the root on the right that means the same thing.

_____ 31. ortho                  A. cede, ceed, cess

_____ 32. soma                   B. hydro

_____ 33. non, nov(em)           C. sol

_____ 34. auto                   D. hypo

_____ 35. aqu(a)                 E. carn

_____ 36. ambu                   F. enne

_____ 37. helio                  G. ego

_____ 38. sub                    H. rect

_____ 39. omni                   I. gog(ue)

_____ 40. arch                   J. pan

# Units 29–32 Quiz

## Matching, Part I

**Directions:** Match each word to its definition.

_____ 1. euphony

_____ 2. monogamy

_____ 3. octagon

_____ 4. genocide

_____ 5. psychosomatic

_____ 6. xenophobia

_____ 7. homogenous

_____ 8. astrology

_____ 9. antithesis

_____ 10. sympathy

A. killing of a race

B. marriage with one person at a time

C. of the same kind

D. the direct opposite

E. study of the stars

F. an object that has eight sides

G. pleasant sounding

H. physical disorder due to mental state

I. feeling that is the same as another

J. fear of strangers

## Matching, Part II

**Directions:** Match each word to its definition.

_____ 11. macroscopic

_____ 12. triarchy

_____ 13. misanthrope

_____ 14. simultaneous

_____ 15. hypothermia

_____ 16. hydrophobia

_____ 17. perihelion

_____ 18. egocentric

_____ 19. phonometer

_____ 20. philanthropy

A. measures the intensity of sound

B. love of mankind

C. hater of mankind

D. visible to the naked eye

E. government or rule by three persons

F. fear of water

G. that point in a planet's orbit path that is closest to the sun around which it travels

H. happening at the same time

I. self-centered

J. condition of reduced temperature

# Units 29–32 Quiz *(cont.)*

## Matching, Part III

**Directions:** Match each word to its definition.

_____ 21. precede

_____ 22. pentagon

_____ 23. heliocentric

_____ 24. astronaut

_____ 25. bibliomania

_____ 26. homochromous

_____ 27. acrophobia

_____ 28. somnambulate

_____ 29. multilingual

_____ 30. tripod

A. fear of heights

B. universe where the sun is the center

C. an interplanetary traveler

D. to speak several languages

E. obsession with books

F. three-legged stand

G. to sleepwalk

H. to come before

I. an object with five sides

J. of the same color

## Matching, Part IV

**Directions:** Match each word to its definition.

_____ 31. carnivore

_____ 32. automotive

_____ 33. narcissistic

_____ 34. fratricide

_____ 35. contemporary

_____ 36. mnemonic

_____ 37. stentorian

_____ 38. mercurial

_____ 39. perennial

_____ 40. malediction

A. extremely loud

B. lasting through the year or through many years

C. the act of killing one's brother

D. curse; "bad speech"

E. moving by itself; self-propelled

F. something that eats meat

G. changeable; swift

H. assisting memory

I. a person living during the same time period as another

J. self-absorbed; exceedingly vain; conceited; in love with oneself

# Answer Key

## Unit 1

*Matching* (p. 10)

| | | |
|---|---|---|
| 1. J | 5. G | 8. C |
| 2. A | 6. F | 9. D |
| 3. I | 7. H | 10. B |
| 4. E | | |

*Definitions* (p. 10)

1. a wise fool; a student in the second year of high school or college
2. fear/hatred of life; life of fear/hatred
3. study of self secrets; study of secret self; study of hidden self
4. love of time; time of love
5. measurement of Earth; a branch of mathematics dealing with properties, relations, and measurements of solids, surfaces, lines, points, and angles

Affix Practice (p. 11)
Affix Meaning: Earth
Verb: none
Adjective: geological
Adverb: geologically
Noun: geology, geologist

## Unit 1 Quiz (pp. 12–13)

1. zoology: logy (root); science of, study of (meaning); the study of animals
2. millimeter: meter (root); unit of measurement (meaning); 1000th of a meter
3. chronological: chrono (root), time (meaning); logy (root), science of, study of (meaning); the study of time (its ordering)
4. arachnophobia: phobia (root); fear, hatred of (meaning); fear of spiders
5. telegram: gram (root); something written (meaning); a written message transmitted over a long distance
6. sophomore: soph (root); wisdom (meaning); more (root), fool (meaning); a knowledgeable fool

7. Helios: helio (root); sun (meaning); the Sun god
8. benephile: phile (root); love (meaning); literally, "love of good"
9. biography: bio (root); life (meaning); graph (root), to write (meaning); a book written about a life (literally, "life writing")

| | | |
|---|---|---|
| 10. C | 14. B | 18. I |
| 11. H | 15. G | 19. H |
| 12. A | 16. D | 20. J |
| 13. E | 17. F | |

## Unit 2

*Matching* (p. 14)

| | | |
|---|---|---|
| 1. B | 5. I | 8. F |
| 2. C | 6. A | 9. H |
| 3. E | 7. D | 10. J |
| 4. G | | |

*Definitions* (p. 15)

1. marriage to oneself; pollination by its own pollen
2. far away measurement; a device for measuring objects that are far away
3. killing of living things; living to kill things
4. study or science of how to write; study/science of handwriting
5. secret, hidden name; to name something in secret

*Affix Practice* (p. 15)
Affix Element: syn
Affix Meaning: same, together with
Verb: none
Adjective: synonymous
Adverb: synonymously
Noun: synonym

## Unit 2 Quiz (pp. 16–17)

1. bigamy: gam (root); marriage (meaning); having two marriages
2. nominate: nom (root); name (meaning); to name (as a candidate)
3. eponym: nym (root); name (meaning); named for itself
4. telephoto lens: tele (root); far (meaning); a lens that allows for the picture-

taking of things that are far away
5. matricide: cide (root); to kill (meaning); the killing of one's mother
6. polygon: poly (root); many (meaning); a many-sided object
7. monarchy: arch (root); first, chief, ancient, ruler of government (meaning); the rule of/by one
8. misguided: mis (root); bad, wrong (meaning); poorly thought out or planned
9. gene: gen (root); birth, race, kind (meaning); that with which we are born that forms who we will become
10. epidemic: dem (root); people (meaning); something that people infect each other with (usually a disease)

| | | |
|---|---|---|
| 11. G | 15. J | 18. I |
| 12. D | 16. C | 19. F |
| 13. A | 17. E | 20. H |
| 14. B | | |

## Unit 3

*Matching* (p. 18)

| | | |
|---|---|---|
| 1. E | 5. F | 8. A |
| 2. H | 6. G | 9. I |
| 3. C | 7. J | 10. B |
| 4. D | | |

*Definitions* (p. 18)

1. self rule; self knowledge
2. measurement of water; a device for measuring water
3. picture; production of an image by the action of light; written light
4. fear/hatred of large stars; large fear/hatred of stars
5. study or science of small life; science of small microorganisms

*Affix Practice* (p. 19)
Affix Element: bene
Affix Meaning: good, well
Verb: benefit, benefited, benefiting
Adjective: beneficial
Adverb: beneficially

Noun: benefit, beneficiary, beneficence

*Extended Activity* (p. 19)
Accept reasonable responses.
Dr. Seuss; Theodore Geisel; *The Cat in the Hat*
Mark Twain; Samuel Longhorne Clemens; *The Adventures of Huckleberry Finn*
George Orwell; Eric Blair; *Animal Farm*
O. Henry; William Sidney Porter; *The Gift of the Magi*

## Unit 3 Quiz (pp. 20–21)

1. microscope: micro (root); small (meaning); a device for seeing the very small
2. pseudopod: pseudo (root); false (meaning); [a creature with a] "false" foot
3. hydroplane: hydro (root); water (meaning); a water plane (i.e., a plane that can take off from and land on water)
4. agronomy: nomy (root); knowledge, rule (meaning); the science of soil management and crop production (literally, "field arrangement")
5. benefactor: bene (root); good, well (meaning); one who does good
6. megalith: mega (root); great, large (meaning); a large stone
7. astronautics: astro (root); star (meaning); the practice of being among the stars
8. pathos: path (root); feelings, sufferings, disease (meaning); feelings that can be felt by others (literally, "same feeling")
9. photocopy: photo (root); light (meaning); a copy made by the use of light
10. phonetic: phon (root); sound (meaning); concerning sound

| | | |
|---|---|---|
| 11. D | 15. B | 18. E |
| 12. G | 16. H | 19. F |
| 13. J | 17. C | 20. I |
| 14. A | | |

# Answer Key *(cont.)*

## Unit 4

*Matching (p. 22)*

| | | | |
|---|---|---|---|
| 1. I | 4. F | 7. J | 9. B |
| 2. D | 5. A | 8. E | 10. G |
| 3. H | 6. C | | |

*Definitions (p. 22)*

1. citizen/city of the world; worldly, sophisticated
2. against feelings/suffering/disease;feeling brought forth through dislike
3. to see around/near; an instrument used when looking around
4. large/great city/citizen; greatest concentration of citizens in one area
5. fear/hatred of fire

*Affix Practice (p. 23)*

Affix Element: none
Verb: politicize
Adjective: political, politic
Adverb: politically
Noun: politics, politician

## Unit 4 Quiz (pp. 24–25)

1. politics: polit (root); city, citizen (meaning); the practice of organizing people
2. antitrust: anti (root); against (meaning); against a trust (in business, a trust is a group put together to defeat competition)
3. horoscope: scop (root); to see (meaning); seeing in time, seeing into the future
4. pyromaniac: pyr (root); fire (meaning); a person crazy concerning fire
5. podiatrist: pod (root); foot (meaning); one who works with feet, a foot doctor
6. hypodermic: hypo (root); under, less than (meaning); something (that goes) under the skin
7. hypercritical: hyper (root); over, excessive (meaning); overly judgmental
8. pericardium: peri (root); around, near (meaning); something near the heart; a sac covering the heart

9. symposium: sym (root); same, together with (meaning); people together to discuss a topic
10. pedicure: ped (root); foot (meaning); care or treatment of the feet

| | | |
|---|---|---|
| 11. C | 15. F | 18. A |
| 12. I | 16. J | 19. H |
| 13. B | 17. G | 20. D |
| 14. E | | |

## Units 1–4 Review (p. 26)

| | | |
|---|---|---|
| 1. V | 13. BB | 25. Q |
| 2. X | 14. H | 26. P |
| 3. A | 15. EE | 27. DD |
| 4. HH | 16. FF | 28. S |
| 5. M | 17. K | 29. Z |
| 6. CC | 18. J | 30. G |
| 7. D | 19. B | 31. T |
| 8. R | 20. L | 32. JJ |
| 9. I | 21. C | 33. N |
| 10. E | 22. F | 34. II |
| 11. W | 23. GG | 35. U |
| 12. AA | 24. O | 36. Y |

## Units 1–4 Quiz

*Matching, Part I (p. 28)*

| | | |
|---|---|---|
| 1. F | 5. E | 8. A |
| 2. J | 6. I | 9. B |
| 3. G | 7. C | 10. D |
| 4. H | | |

*Matching, Part II (p. 28)*

| | | |
|---|---|---|
| 11. F | 15. G | 18. D |
| 12. I | 16. J | 19. E |
| 13. H | 17. C | 20. A |
| 14. B | | |

*Matching, Part III (p. 29)*

| | | |
|---|---|---|
| 21. G | 26. F | 31. J |
| 22. A | 27. L | 32. O |
| 23. I | 28. B | 33. C |
| 24. K | 29. N | 34. E |
| 25. M | 30. D | 35. H |

## Unit 5

*Matching (p. 32)*

| | | |
|---|---|---|
| 1. B | 5. G | 8. D |
| 2. C | 6. I | 9. F |
| 3. E | 7. H | 10. J |
| 4. A | | |

*Defijnitions (p. 33)*

1. occurring every seven years; happening seven times a year

2. government of three people (men); body of three persons
3. every 10 years
4. musical group of six; group of six
5. mythical animal with one horn
6. nine-sided figure; a polygon with nine sides; nine angles, corners
7. eighth month of Roman calendar; 10th month of Gregorian calendar
8. copy of something; two of something
9. marriage to two people at the same time; act of marrying one person while still married to another
10. something that is three-footed; a camera stand

*Extended Activity (p. 33)*

The first 100 years (1–100) represented the first century.

## Unit 5 Quiz (pp. 34–35)

1. September: sept (root); seven (meaning); the seventh month of the year (in the original Roman calendar)
2. pentadactyl: penta (root); five (meaning); having five toes or fingers, an animal with this
3. unicycle: uni (root); one (meaning); a one-wheeled vehicle
4. triad: tri (root); three (meaning); a group of three
5. quadruplets: quad (root); four (meaning); four children born at the same time to the same mother
6. binoculars: bi (root); two (meaning); something with two lenses to aid in seeing
7. hexagon: hex (root); six (meaning); a six-sided figure
8. decathlon: dec (root); ten (meaning); an event (in the sport of track and field) with 10 parts

9. quintuplets: quin (root); five (meaning); five children born at the same time to the same mother
10. duel: du (root); two (meaning); a fight concerning two people

| | | |
|---|---|---|
| 11. C | 15. H | 18. E |
| 12. J | 16. D | 19. F |
| 13. G | 17. B | 20. I |
| 14. A | | |

## Unit 6

*Matching (p. 36)*

| | | |
|---|---|---|
| 1. F | 5. I | 8. D |
| 2. E | 6. J | 9. C |
| 3. B | 7. A | 10. H |
| 4. G | | |

*Definitions (p. 36)*

1. many languages; knowing or using several languages
2. equal sides
3. half moon
4. thoughts, feelings spoken alone; the act of talking to oneself
5. 1,000 years

*Affix Practice (p. 37)*

Affix Element: omni
Affix Meaning: all
Verb: none
Adjective: omnivorous
Adverb: omnivorously
Noun: omnivore

## Unit 6 Quiz (pp. 38–39)

1. omnidirectional: omni (root); all (meaning); concerning all directions
2. equivalent: equi (root); equal (meaning); equal
3. multitude: multi (root); many (meaning); many
4. semisweet: semi (root); half (meaning); partially sweet
5. solidarity: sol (root); alone (meaning); togetherness
6. hemistich: hemi (root); half (meaning); half of a line of verse
7. milliliter: mill (root); thousand (meaning); 1000th of a liter

# Answer Key (cont.)

8. kiloton: kilo (root); thousand (meaning); an explosive unit equal to 1,000 tons of TNT

9. centigrade: cent (root); hundred (meaning); having a scale of 100 degrees (e.g., the Celsius scale, on which water boils at 100 degrees)

10. demirelief: demi (root); half (meaning); in sculpture, figures which project halfway out from the background

11. B    15. A    18. J
12. E    16. F    19. I
13. G    17. C    20. D
14. H

## Unit 7

*Matching* (p. 40)

1. J    5. E    8. D
2. H    6. C    9. B
3. G    7. A    10. I
4. F

*Definitions* (p. 40)

1. water city; city of water; citizen of water

2. to "look around"; thoughtful of potential consequences

3. taking off the head; beheading

4. chili with meat

5. hearing something spoken; spoken sound; a machine used for listening to recorded sounds

*Affix Practice* (p. 41)
Affix Element: pre
Affix Meaning: before
Verb: predict
Adjective: predictable
Adverb: predictably
Noun: prediction, predictability

## Unit 7 Quiz (pp. 42–43)

1. dictator: dict (root); to say, speak (meaning); one who says what is to be written or done; in politics, an absolute ruler

2. viaduct: duct (root); to lead (meaning); a structure for carrying a road

or way across something (such as a valley)

3. circumvent: circum (root); around (meaning); to go around

4. aquacade: aqua (root); water (meaning); an exhibition of different activities done in the water

5. recapitulate: cap (root); head (meaning); to state again; to go over again

6. malady: mal (root); bad (meaning); a bad condition, a sickness

7. reincarnation: carn (root); flesh (meaning); to be made flesh again; to be born again, something that is born again

8. prescribe: scrib (root); write (meaning); to advise in writing (usually in medicine)

9. corporal: corp (root); body (meaning); of the body

10. retrospect: spec (root); to see, look (meaning); concerning looking backwards (in time)

11. E    15. A    18. F
12. J    16. G    19. D
13. I    17. B    20. C
14. H

## Unit 8

*Matching* (p. 44)

1. F    5. J    8. E
2. C    6. B    9. D
3. I    7. H    10. A
4. G

*Definitions* (p. 44)

1. government of three people (men)

2. "writing of the heart"; instrument used to record movements of heart

3. one who educates children; a strict teacher

4. rule by religious authority

5. killing of one's father

*Affix Practice* (p. 45)
Affix Element: none
Verb: none
Adjective: maternal

Adverb: maternally
Noun: maternity

*Extended Activity* (p. 45)

1. maid of honor

2. fraternal twins aren't identical

## Unit 8 Quiz (pp. 46–47)

1. pedodontics: ped (root); child (meaning); the practice of caring for children's teeth

2. enamored: amor (root); love (meaning); in love

3. matrilocal: matr (root); mother (meaning); a marriage custom in which the groom goes to live with the bride's family

4. virtuoso: virt (root); man (meaning); a person highly skilled or knowledgeable in a fine art

5. sororate: sor (root); sister (meaning); the custom of a man marrying his wife's sister if his wife dies or is infertile

6. gynecologist: gyn (root); woman (meaning); a doctor concerned with the female reproductive system

7. fraternization: frat (root); brother (meaning); people behaving as brothers, people associating with each other intimately

8. patriarch: pat (root); father (meaning); a man who is head of a family or group

9. monotheism: the (root); god (meaning); the belief in one god

10. cardiac arrest: card (root); heart (meaning); the stopping of the heart

11. C    15. J    18. A
12. D    16. I    19. F
13. B    17. E    20. H
14. G

## Units 5–8 Review (p. 48)

1. N    19. QQ    36. WW
2. OO   20. KK    37. XX
3. P    21. BB    38. DD

4. YY    22. D     39. NN
5. HH    23. V     40. RR
6. K     24. Y     41. VV
7. CC    25. II    42. F
8. H     26. ZZ    43. UU
9. Q     27. J     44. S
10. PP   28. E     45. M
11. SS   29. T     46. G
12. A    30. FF    47. LL
13. U    31. R     48. Z
14. B    32. MM    49. EE
15. X    33. GG    50. C
16. I    34. AA    51. W
17. JJ   35. O     52. L
18. TT

## Units 5–8 Quiz

*Matching, Part I* (p. 50)

1. I    6. N    11. G
2. C    7. L    12. A
3. E    8. B    13. O
4. M    9. J    14. D
5. K    10. F   15. H

*Matching, Part II* (p. 50)

16. E    20. H    23. I
17. J    21. A    24. F
18. C    22. G    25. B
19. D

*True or False* (p. 51)

26. true

27. false; The Capitol is a building; a capital is a head city.

28. false; The pentathlon is made up of five events.

29. false; Dioxide is made up of two oxygen atoms.

30. true

31. true

32. true

33. false; Pediatrics is a branch of medicine that deals with children.

34. true

35. true

*Fill in the Blank* (p. 51)

36. Demigod

37. polygamy

38. valediction

39. conspicuous

# Answer Key (cont.)

40. pericardium
41. quart
42. solo
43. Sororicide
44. tricycle
45. triumvirate
46. duplex
47. heptameter
48. million
49. November
50. prediction

## Unit 9

*Matching* (p.54)

| | | |
|---|---|---|
| 1. C | 5. J | 8. E |
| 2. F | 6. I | 9. G |
| 3. H | 7. A | 10. B |
| 4. D | | |

*Definitions* (p. 54)

1. sufferings, disease, feelings of the mind; person with antisocial behavior
2. book of writing; to write a book; a list of books used in research
3. a device for measuring breathing
4. same name; words with same sound or same spelling, different meanings
5. study of good; something spoken at a funeral

*Affix Practice* (p. 55)

Affix Element: im
Affix Meaning: in, into, within
Verb: import
Adjective: important
Adverb: importantly
Noun: import, importance

## Unit 9 Quiz (pp. 56–57)

1. bibliomania: biblio (root); book (meaning); a craziness for books
2. homogenize: homo (root); same (meaning); to make into parts that are all of the same kind
3. manacle: man (root); hand (meaning); something that holds the hands (e.g., handcuffs)
4. euphemism: euph (root); good, well (meaning); a good or nice phrase for something that isn't so good
5. deportation: port (root); to bring, carry (meaning); forceful expelling from the country
6. factual: fac (root); to make, do (meaning); true, real
7. ventriloquist: loqu (root); to say, speak (meaning); one who speaks not from his/her mouth (literally, "from the belly")
8. psychiatry: psych (root); mind (meaning); the medical practice of treating the mind
9. inspiration: spir (root); to breathe (meaning); something that compels one to do something (literally, "to put breath in")
10. translucent: trans (root); across (meaning); letting light pass through

| | | | |
|---|---|---|---|
| 11. A | 14. C | 17. J | 19. D |
| 12. G | 15. H | 18. B | 20. F |
| 13. E | 16. I | | |

## Unit 10

*Matching* (p. 58)

| | | | |
|---|---|---|---|
| 1. A | 4. B | 7. J | 9. I |
| 2. E | 5. F | 8. H | 10. D |
| 3. C | 6. G | | |

*Definitions* (p. 58)

1. to send between; a recess, break
2. under the skin; a needle used to inject under the skin
3. one who educates children; teacher; ruler of children
4. study of beliefs, opinions; hymns sung at church
5. feelings

*Affix Practice* (p. 59)

Affix Element: dis
Affix Meaning: not, apart
Verb: dissent
Adjective: dissenting
Adverb: none
Noun: dissenter, dissension

*Extended Activity* (page 59)

1. Latin: "friend of the court"
2. Latin: "body of the crime"

3. Latin: "after the fact"

## Unit 10 Quiz (pp. 60–61)

1. infidel: fid (root); faith (meaning); one who is unfaithful
2. orthodox: dox (root); opinion, belief (meaning); that which is accepted as correct or right (literally, "right opinions")
3. hypnagogic: gog (root); ruler, leader (meaning); that which is led or guided by (what is in) sleep
4. permit: mit (root); send (meaning); to allow
5. proclaim: pro (root); forward (meaning); to state loudly
6. ectoderm: derm (root); skin (meaning); the outermost layer of an embryo in early development (literally, "the outermost skin")
7. adjacent: jac (root); throw, hurl (meaning); lying near (literally, "thrown near")
8. gradual: grad (root); to move, to go (meaning); slow
9. insensitive: sens (root); feel (meaning); unfeeling
10. tempo: temp (root); time (meaning); speed, pace

| | | |
|---|---|---|
| 11. D | 15. C | 18. E |
| 12. G | 16. J | 19. H |
| 13. I | 17. F | 20. A |
| 14. B | | |

## Unit 11

*Matching* (p. 62)

| | | |
|---|---|---|
| 1. G | 5. J | 8. B |
| 2. I | 6. C | 9. F |
| 3. A | 7. H | 10. E |
| 4. D | | |

*Definitions* (p. 62)

1. a person who navigates a spacecraft
2. a large block of stone used in architecture, sculpture
3. half moon
4. a written description of animals and habitats
5. under the sea; machine operating under water

*Affix Practice* (p. 63)

Affix Element: in
Affix Meaning: without, not
Verb: none
Adjective: incredible, incredulous
Adverb: incredibly, incredulously
Noun: incredibility, incredulity

*Extended Activity* (p. 63)

1. merman
2. Answers will vary.

## Unit 11 Quiz (pp. 64–65)

1. lunatic: lun (root); moon (meaning); a crazy person (literally, a moon person (as in someone made crazy by the moon)
2. discreditable: cred (root); to believe (meaning); something that can be shown to be unbelievable
3. aquamarine: aqua (root); sea (meaning); a light bluish-green; a stone that has this color
4. lithographic: lith (root); stone (meaning); prints or writing made by using a process involving a stone surface
5. semiannual: ann (root); year (meaning); half-yearly
6. bicentennial: enn (root); year (meaning); happening every 200 years; lasting 200 years
7. solar system: sol (root); sun (meaning); a planetary system revolving around a star
8. verbatim: verb (root); word (meaning); said or reading exactly
9. nauseous: nau (root); ship (meaning); feeling like one is going to vomit (e.g., seasickness)
10. zoology: zoo (root); animal (meaning); the study of animals

| | | |
|---|---|---|
| 11. C | 15. I | 18. E |
| 12. G | 16. J | 19. B |
| 13. H | 17. D | 20. A |
| 14. F | | |

# Answer Key (cont.)

## Unit 12

*Matching* (p. 66)

| | | |
|---|---|---|
| 1. A | 5. I | 8. F |
| 2. C | 6. J | 9. D |
| 3. E | 7. H | 10. B |
| 4. G | | |

*Definitions* (p. 66)

1. to eat all; one who takes in everything available
2. middle skin; the layer of skin between ectoderm and endoderm
3. government by the clergy
4. large, great world or universe; the entire world, universe
5. those assembled for a performance; the act of hearing a performance

*Affix Practice* (p. 67)

Affix Element: re
Affix Meaning: back, again
Verb: recede
Adjective: recessive, recessional
Adverb: recessively
Noun: recess, recession

### Unit 12 Quiz (pp. 68–69)

1. cryosurgery: cryo (root); cold (meaning); a medical operation performed involving extreme cold
2. mesosphere: meso (root); middle (meaning); the middle layer of the atmosphere
3. excessive: cess (root); to go (meaning); gone too far, overly much
4. auditorium: aud (root); to hear, hearing, sound (meaning); a place that people gather to hear or see something (such as a speaker, etc.)
5. cosmopolitan: cosm (root); world, universe (meaning); educated, experienced (literally, "that which pertains to worldly people")
6. precognition: cogn (root); to learn (meaning); something thought or known in advance
7. inquest: ques (root); to ask, to seek (meaning); an investigation
8. hieroglyphics: hier (root), holy, sacred (meaning); writing in the form of pictures or carvings (literally, "concerning sacred carvings")
9. macrophage: macro (root), large, great (meaning); a type of white blood cell (literally, "something that eats large things")
10. herbivore: vor (root), to eat (meaning); something that eats (only) plants

| | | | |
|---|---|---|---|
| 11. H | 14. A | 17. C | 19. E |
| 12. D | 15. I | 18. B | 20. F |
| 13. J | 16. G | | |

## Units 9–12 Review (p. 70)

| | | |
|---|---|---|
| 1. H | 18. P | 35. LL |
| 2. W | 19. N | 36. GG |
| 3. SS | 20. HH | 37. D |
| 4. DD | 21. C | 38. X |
| 5. U | 22. S | 39. CC |
| 6. M | 23. II | 40. UU |
| 7. Y | 24. EE | 41. WW |
| 8. L | 25. G | 42. E |
| 9. JJ | 26. VV | 43. PP |
| 10. RR | 27. T | 44. OO |
| 11. AA | 28. R | 45. I |
| 12. F | 29. KK | 46. O |
| 13. B | 30. XX | 47. Q |
| 14. A | 31. TT | 48. J |
| 15. K | 32. QQ | 49. FF |
| 16. V | 33. MM | 50. BB |
| 17. Z | 34. NN | |

## Unit 14

*Matching* (p. 74)

| | | |
|---|---|---|
| 1. G | 11. D | 21. CC |
| 2. BB | 12. K | 22. C |
| 3. B | 13. T | 23. N |
| 4. F | 14. F | 24. H |
| 5. R | 15. J | 25. O |
| 6. W | 16. Y | 26. U |
| 7. L | 17. E | 27. AA |
| 8. M | 18. Q | 28. A |
| 9. S | 19. X | 29. I |
| 10. Z | 20. V | 30. P |

## Unit 15

*Matching* (p. 75)

| | | |
|---|---|---|
| 1. X | 11. K | 20. Z |
| 2. W | 12. L | 21. B |
| 3. T | 13. O | 22. AA |
| 4. M | 14. R | 23. D |
| 5. E | 15. U | 24. F |
| 6. J | 16. G | 25. BB |
| 7. S | 17. P | 26. I |
| 8. A | 18. V | 27. H |
| 9. C | 19. N | 28. Y |
| 10. Q | | |

## Unit 16

*Word Trees* (p. 76)
Answers will vary.

## Unit 17

*Matching* (p. 80)

| | | | |
|---|---|---|---|
| 1. E | 4. H | 7. D | 9. G |
| 2. F | 5. B | 8. I | 10. A |
| 3. C | 6. J | | |

*Definitions* (p. 81)

1. strand of DNA that carries genes
2. good, well wish; a desire to perform generous acts
3. different birth, kind, or race; consisting of dissimilar parts
4. foot healing; medicine dealing with feet
5. applied science, study; science of industrial, commercial objectives

*Affix Practice* (p. 81)

Affix Element: ex
Affix Meaning: outside of, away from
Verb: exclaim
Adjective: exclamatory
Adverb: none
Noun: exclamation, exclaimer

*Extended Activity* (p. 81)

Answers will vary:
row, bass, wound, refuse, read, lead, live, desert, produce, etc.

### Unit 17 Quiz (pp. 82–83)

1. chromosphere: chrom (root); color (meaning); a gaseous layer of the sun's atmosphere
2. appendage: pend (root); hanging, weigh (meaning); something that hangs off a body (e.g., arm, leg)
3. technical: tech (root); skill, craft (meaning); of or relating to a particular subject or craft
4. pediatrics: iatr (root); healing, medicine (meaning); (medicine) concerning children
5. volunteer: vol (root); wish (meaning); one who does something by choice
6. heterodox: hetero (root); other, another, different (meaning); of different or unusual opinions, beliefs, etc.
7. direction: rect (root); straight (meaning); guidance, instruction
8. egocentric: ego (root); self, I (meaning); centered around oneself
9. somatogenic: soma (root); body, flesh (meaning); originating in the cells of the human body
10. reclamation: clam (root); to cry out (meaning); taking back; taking again

| | | |
|---|---|---|
| 11. C | 15. H | 18. D |
| 12. F | 16. B | 19. E |
| 13. A | 17. J | 20. G |
| 14. I | | |

## Unit 18

*Matching* (p. 84)

| | | | |
|---|---|---|---|
| 1. E | 4. I | 7. D | 9. F |
| 2. H | 5. B | 8. J | 10. A |
| 3. C | 6. G | | |

*Definitions* (p. 85)

1. under, below Earth; hidden, secret; operating beneath Earth's surface
2. after graduation; person pursuing advanced study after graduation
3. talking backward; speaking of the past
4. turning things into form of man, human
5. straight child, straight foot; medicine that deals with injuries of skeletal system

# Answer Key *(cont.)*

6. televised or seen images

7. nine-sided figure; nine angles, corners

8. plant eater

9. aliens; occurring outside of Earth

10. many forms, shapes; different forms of the same species

**Unit 18 Quiz (pp. 86–87)**

1. postpone: post (root); after (meaning); to delay (literally, "in a place after")

2. terrain: terr (root); earth (meaning); land, ground, earth

3. videlicet: vid (root); to see (meaning); namely (literally, "see [that] it is permissible")

4. herbage: herb (root); plant (meaning); plant life

5. diagonal: gon (root); corner, angle, side (meaning); a direction slanting across

6. retrovirus: retro (root); backward (meaning); a type of virus that inserts a copy of its DNA in the host cell (literally, a virus that works backwards)

7. orthodontia: ortho (root); straight (meaning); the practice of making teeth right or straight

8. episode: epi (root); on, upon (meaning); an event or happening

9. morphologist: morph (root); form, shape (meaning); one who studies the forms of things

10. subsonic: sub (root); under, below (meaning); relating to speeds slower than sound

11. E  14. G  17. C  19. D
12. A  15. H  18. I  20. F
13. J  16. B

**Unit 19**

*Matching* (p. 88)

1. A  4. H  7. B  9. I
2. E  5. J  8. G  10. D
3. F  6. C

*Definitions* (p. 88)

1. able to use both hands equally well

2. of or relating to the Middle Ages

3. unselfish; incredibly courageous in mind and heart

4. relating to infants; newly born

5. person who delivers flowers, cares for flowers

*Affix Practice* (p. 89)
Affix Element: dis
Affix Meaning: out
Verb: dissimulate
Adjective: dissimilar
Adverb: dissimilarly
Noun: dissimilarity, dissimulation
*Extended Activity* (p. 89)
nonflammable

**Unit 19 Quiz (pp. 90–91)**

1. median: med (root); middle (meaning); the middle

2. documentary: doc (root); to teach (meaning); a film (etc.) that teaches (usually about a particular person or event)

3. amphibious: amphi (root); both (meaning); suited for both land and water, having a twofold nature

4. native: nat (root); to be born (meaning); having been born to a particular place (etc.)

5. animation: anim (root); life, spirit (meaning); bringing to life; drawings "brought to life" (i.e., made to appear to move)

6. simile: simil (root); same, like (meaning); a figure of speech comparing something to something else using "like" or "as"

7. flora: flor (root); flower (meaning); plant life (literally, "flowers")

8. erroneous: err (root); to wander (meaning); wrong, mistaken

9. amnesiac: mne (root); to remember (meaning); one who has no memory (or has lost some memory)

10. nonflammable: flam (root); fire (meaning); cannot be set on fire; cannot be burned

11. D  14. J  17. A  19. E
12. F  15. I  18. B  20. H
13. G  16. C

**Unit 20**
*Matching* (p. 92)

1. D  4. F  7. C
2. H  5. G  8. E
3. A  6. B  9. I

*Definitions* (p.92)

10. to climb above the limits of; climb across

11. after war

12. fear of closed, enclosed, shut spaces

13. a straight line passing through the center of a body; to measure across, through

14. to use misleading language; equally calling out

15. exceeding the usual or required number

*Affix Practice* (p. 93)
Affix Element: super
Affix Meaning: above, beyond
Verb: supervise
Adjective: supervisory
Adverb: none
Noun: supervision, supervisor
*Extended Activity* (p. 93)
Accept reasonable responses.

**Unit 20 Quiz (pp. 94–95)**

1. dial: dia (root); across, through (meaning); the face of a clock, watch, etc.; a knob that can be turned

2. false: fal (root); to deceive (meaning); not true, fake

3. ascend: scend (root); to climb (meaning); go upwards

4. claustrophobia: claus (root); to shut, close (meaning); fear of closed-in spaces

5. supervision: super (root); above, beyond (meaning); the act of looking or watching over (work, behavior, etc.)

6. cyclical: cycl (root); circle (meaning); circular (literally, "that which goes around")

7. cadence: cad (root); fall (meaning); a fall in pitch, esp. at the end of a phrase; rhythm

8. include: clud (root); to shut, close (meaning); to give in addition to; add, enclose

9. bellicose: belli (root); war (meaning); war-like; angry

10. vocative: voc (root); to call out (meaning); capable of speaking or calling out

11. E  14. I  17. C  19. J
12. D  15. A  18. B  20. G
13. H  16. F

**Units 17–20 Review (p. 96)**

1. U    15. HH   28. Y
2. V    16. W    29. II
3. LL   17. CC   30. D
4. C    18. T    31. FF
5. E    19. F    32. M
6. EE   20. AA   33. H
7. KK   21. BB   34. X
8. A    22. S    35. N
9. Z    23. GG   36. MM
10. K   24. Q    37. P
11. B   25. G    38. O
12. R   26. I    39. NN
13. DD  27. L    40. J
14. JJ

**Unit 21**

*Matching* (p. 100)

1. E  3. B  5. G  7. A
2. C  4. F  6. D

*Definitions* (p. 100)

8. changeable, swift; from Mercury (Hermes), Latin

9. requiring tremendous strength; from Hercules, Greco-Roman

10. gloomy, taciturn; from Saturn (Cronus), Roman

11. a deadly adversary; from Nemesis, Greek

12. jolly, hearty; from Jupiter (Jove, Zeus), Latin, Italian

13. to torment with unattainable things; Tantalus, son of Zeus, Greek

14. powerful, huge; Titans, giant overthrown by Olympian gods, Greek

15. self-absorbed, exceedingly vain; Narcissus, youth who fell in love with himself, Greek

## Unit 22

*Matching (p. 101)*

| | | |
|---|---|---|
| 1. B | 5. G | 9. F |
| 2. E | 6. A | 10. I |
| 3. H | 7. J | 11. D |
| 4. K | 8. L | 12. C |

*Definitions (p. 101)*

13. an induced sleep-like condition; Hypnos, god of sleep, Greek

14. a sudden, overpowering, contagious terror; Pan, Greek

15. producing an array of rainbow-like colors; Iris, Greek

16. insane; Luna, moon goddess, Latin

17. extremely loud; Stentor, from *The Iliad*, Greek

## Unit 23

*Matching (p. 102)*

| | | |
|---|---|---|
| 1. L | 5. A | 9. I |
| 2. B | 6. J | 10. G |
| 3. E | 7. K | 11. C |
| 4. F | 8. D | 12. H |

*Definitions (p. 102)*

13. sleepwalking; Somnus, god of sleep, Latin

14. a woven, knitted pressed fabric of fibrous material; Clotho, one of the Fates, Old English

15. science of good health; Hygeia, goddess of health, Greek

16. any grain used for food; Ceres, goddess of agriculture, Latin

17. relating to drama, actor, actress; Thespis, Greek

## Unit 24

*Matching (p. 103)*

| | | |
|---|---|---|
| 1. I | 4. G | 7. E |
| 2. F | 5. H | 8. A |
| 3. B | 6. D | 9. C |

*Definitions (p. 101)*

10. an unconfirmed report; Rumor, Latin, Old English

11. a form of energy generated by friction, induction, chemical, radiant effects; Electra, Greek, Latin

12. a vent in Earth's crust through which rocks, dust, ash, or molten rock in the form of liquid magma is ejected; Vulcan, god of fire, Latin, Italian

13. something that is reborn from its own destruction, a bird consumed by fire that rises from the ashes; Greek

14. the upper, main part of the brain of vertebrate animals; Cereberus, Latin

15. group of arthropods with four pairs of legs, lung-like sacs, breathing tubes, and a body divided into two segments; Arachne, Greek

16. the repeating sound produced by reflection of sound waves from a surface; Echo, a nymph punished by Hera, Greek, French, Latin

*Extended Activity (p. 103)*

Achilles' mother Thetis dipped him in the River Styx to protect him from harm. However, the water didn't touch his heel at which she held him, so he remained vulnerable at that one spot.

## Units 21–24 Quiz

*Matching, Part I (p. 104)*

| | | |
|---|---|---|
| 1. F | 5. C | 8. D |
| 2. B | 6. I | 9. A |
| 3. H | 7. J | 10. G |
| 4. E | | |

*Matching, Part II (p. 105)*

| | | |
|---|---|---|
| 11. S | 16. K | 21. Q |
| 12. N | 17. M | 22. L |
| 13. U | 18. T | 23. O |
| 14. X | 19. Y | 24. P |
| 15. R | 20. V | 25. W |

## Unit 25

*Matching (p. 108)*

| | | |
|---|---|---|
| 1. B | 5. C | 8. F |
| 2. E | 6. J | 9. A |
| 3. G | 7. I | 10. D |
| 4. H | | |

*Definitions (p. 108)*

1. after birth, following childbirth

2. fear or hatred of heights

3. the killing of a king

4. having total knowledge, knowing everything

5. action on one another

*Affix Practice (p. 109)*

Affix Element: dis

Affix Meaning: not, opposite of, absence

Verb: disrupt

Adjective: disruptive

Adverb: disruptively

Noun: disruption, disrupter

*Extended Activity (p. 109)*

Answers will vary. Some examples are AIDS, scuba, MADD, Nascar, etc.

## Unit 25 Quiz (pp. 110–111)

1. intercept: inter (root); between (meaning); to take while [something is] traveling between

2. scientist: sci (root); to know (meaning); one who knows (about some aspect of the physical world)

3. suffix: fix (root); to fasten (meaning); a word ending (literally, "fastened underneath")

4. necrosis: necro (root); corpse (meaning); the death of tissue (caused by disease or injury)

5. ergonomic: erg (root); work (meaning); concerning efficiency in working

6. tyrannosaurus rex: rex (root); king (meaning); a top predator among the dinosaurs (literally, "terrible lizard king")

7. acrophobia: acro (root); topmost, high (meaning); fear of heights

8. parentage: par (root); to give birth to (meaning); concerning who has given birth to another

9. corrupt: rupt (root); to break (meaning); wicked, unjust; impure (literally, "broken with")

10. regimen: reg (root); king (meaning); a way of living, eating, exercising, etc. (which one is "ruled" by)

| | | |
|---|---|---|
| 11. B | 15. C | 18. A |
| 12. F | 16. J | 19. E |
| 13. G | 17. D | 20. H |
| 14. I | | |

## Unit 26

*Matching (p. 112)*

| | | |
|---|---|---|
| 1. C | 5. J | 8. H |
| 2. D | 6. F | 9. I |
| 3. G | 7. B | 10. E |
| 4. A | | |

*Definitions (p. 113)*

1. one who opposes, a principal character's opposition; struggle against

2. the physics of the relationships between heat and other forms of energy

3. identity of musical pitch; a combination of musical parts with same pitch

4. to combine separate elements or substances to form a coherent whole

5. the belief that God and nature are one

6. passing to successive generations only in females; whole woman

7. characteristic of the beginning of Stone Ages; first stone

8. in, within the heart; the thin membrane that lines the interior of the heart

# Answer Key (cont.)

9. extraterrestrial biology; study of outside life
10. a celestial being next in rank above angel; chief angel, first messenger

*Extended Activity* (p. 113)

A preacher who spreads his or her message via television.

## Unit 26 Quiz (pp. 114–115)

1. evangelical: angel (root); messenger (meaning); of or according to the teachings of the gospels (literally, "from good news of angels")
2. agony: agon (root); struggle (meaning); great pain or suffering
3. epithet: the (root); to put, place (meaning); a type of word describing something (usually negatively)
4. exotic: exo (root); out of, outside (meaning); outside of the normal; unusual, foreign
5. sonic boom: son (root); hearing, sound (meaning); a low crack made when something traveling faster than sound passes by
6. protolithic: proto (root); first (meaning); of the earliest Stone Age (literally, "of the first stone")
7. dynamite: dyna (root); power (meaning); a type of powerful explosive
8. Holocene: holo (root); whole (meaning); the period in history marked by the development of human culture (literally, "wholly new")
9. pantomime: pan (root); all (meaning); the use of only gestures and facial expressions to indicate meaning
10. endocrine: endo (root); in, into, within (meaning); secreting directly into the blood (literally, "sifting inside")

11. F   14. G   17. C   19. A
12. B   15. D   18. H   20. E
13. J   16. I

## Unit 27

*Matching* (p. 116)

1. B    5. I    8. E
2. G    6. A    9. D
3. J    7. F    10. C
4. H

*Definitions* (p. 116)

1. a typewritten copy of a manuscript
2. relating to the equinox; night and day are the same length
3. a person who mixes drinks; a person who studies mixing; a bartender
4. foreign, strange love; love of foreign things
5. a person new to a field or activity; beginner; a person who's religious but hasn't taken vows

*Affix Practice* (p. 117)

Affix Element: de
Affix Meaning: reverse, remove, reduce
Verb: defend
Adjective: defendable, defensive, defensible
Adverb: defensively, defensibly
Noun: defendant, defense, defensiveness

*Extended Activity* (p. 117)

1. Wow! I can't believe my luck!
2. Since school ends on May 30th, my parents planned our summer vacation for the second week in June.
3. "Is Janie coming with us?" asked Samantha.
4. My chores include the following: washing and putting away dishes, dusting and sweeping my bedroom, and taking out the garbage.
5. Planes, Trains, and Automobiles is my favorite movie of all time, and "It Might Be You" is my favorite song.

## Unit 27 Quiz (pp. 118–119)

1. kleptomania: mania (root); madness (meaning); the intense desire to steal (literally, "thief craziness")
2. extraordinary: ord (root); order (meaning); beyond normal
3. xenophilia: xeno (root); strange, foreign (meaning); the love of things foreign
4. nocturne: noct (root); night (meaning); a short musical piece of a romantic nature; a picture of a night scene
5. typify: type (root); blow, impression (meaning); to be an example of
6. mixed-media: mix (root); to mix (meaning); a piece of art, etc., composed of differing type (for example, a statue that plays music)
7. novelty: nov (root); new (meaning); something that is new or unique
8. compunctions: punc (root); to stab, point (meaning); feelings of guilt or regret (literally, "pricks with" or "stabbings with")
9. offensive: fen (root); to ward, strike off (meaning); meant to insult; aggressive, attacking
10. designate: sign (root); sign, seal, mark (meaning); name, appoint, specify (literally, "to mark")

11. D   15. I   18. J
12. F   16. B   19. E
13. A   17. C   20. G
14. H

## Unit 28

*Matching* (p. 120)

1. C    5. D    8. J
2. A    6. F    9. I
3. B    7. G    10. H
4. E

*Definitions* (p. 120)

11. to speak against, to speak the opposite
12. to identify, present, acquaint; to lead within
13. generous and noble in forgiving; large, great spirit or life
14. the act of multiplying; the act of increasing in amount; many folds
15. moving or lying in same plane; corresponding

*Affix Practice* (p. 121)

Affix Element: re
Affix Meaning: back, again
Verb: reflect
Adjective: reflective, reflexive, reflex
Adverb: reflectively, reflexively
Noun: reflection, reflector, reflex

*Extended Activity* (p. 121)

summa cum laude or valedictorian

## Unit 28 Quiz (pp. 122–123)

1. comply: ply (root); to fold, bend (meaning); go along with
2. motive: mot (root); to move (meaning); the reason for doing something (literally, "that which moves")
3. paralegal: para (root); alongside (meaning); one who aids someone else in the practice of law
4. genuflect: flect (root); to bend, twist (meaning); to bend, esp. as a sign of worship or respect (literally, "knee bend")
5. minute: min (root); small (meaning); very small
6. contraband: contra (root); against, opposite (meaning); that which is against the rules or law (literally, "proclamation against")
7. ambulatory: ambu (root); to go, to walk (meaning); capable of movement
8. mortgage: mort (root); death (meaning); giving the rights of a property to a creditor to secure the future payment of a debt (literally, "dead pledge")
9. irresolute: solut (root); free, loosen (meaning); unsure, hesitant, undecided (literally, "not resolved")

# Answer Key *(cont.)*

10. presentiment: pre (root), before (meaning); a feeling regarding something that will happen in the future
11. D          17. A
12. L          18. H
13. K          19. I
14. F          20. G
15. E          21. C
16. J          22. B

**Unit 25–28 Review (p. 124)**
1. D           21. R
2. Y           22. S
3. Z           23. EE
4. CC          24. P
5. DD          25. HH
6. BB          26. GG
7. W           27. E
8. FF          28. G
9. H           29. X
10. V          30. AA
11. M          31. F
12. KK         32. II
13. J          33. C
14. O          34. A
15. LL         35. B
16. NN         36. JJ
17. I          37. MM
18. Q          38. N
19. T          39. K
20. U          40. L

**Unit 29**
*Which One Doesn't Belong?* (p. 126)
1. gynecologist
2. automaton
3. inspection
4. moronic
5. lithography

*True or False* (p. 126)
6. false; Theology is the study of gods.
7. false; Omnivores are all-eating animals. It's also a person who devours knowledge.
8. true
9. false; Millipedes have 1,000 legs.
10. true

*Combining Roots* (p. 127)
11. word: pseudopod; definition: false foot
12. word: phobophobia; definition: fear/hatred of fear/hatred
13. word: pentagon; definition: five-sided figure (five corner, five angles)
14. word: aquapolis; definition: water city/citizen; city/citizen of water
15. word: ichythyology; definition: study of fish

*Word Tree* (p. 127)
Accept reasonable responses.

**Unit 30**
*Matching* (p. 128)
1. F      5. H      8. A
2. E      6. J      9. B
3. G      7. I      10. D
4. C

*Which One Doesn't Belong?* (p. 128)
11. meteorology
12. demigod
13. spectator
14. tetrahedron
15. transport

*True or False* (p. 129)
16. false; November is the ninth month.
17. true
18. false; A microscope sees small things. Micrometer can be used to measure small distances.
19. false; A microcosm is a small world or universe. A macrocosm is a large world or universe.
20. true

*Word Tree* (p. 129)
Answers will vary. Accept reasonable responses.
Suggested answers for first word tree—
Word 1: telescope
Word 2A: microscope
Word 2B: telephone
Word 3A: microcosm
Word 3B: microphone
Word 3C: telegram

Suggested answers for second word tree—
Word 1: unicycle
Word 2A: unilateral
Word 2B: bicycle
Word 3A: unicorn
Word 3B: bilateral
Word 3C: motorcycle

**Unit 31**
*True or False* (p. 130)
1. true
2. false; Photograph technically means "written light."
3. false; Dual personalities are two.
4. true
5. true

*Semi, Demi, or Hemi?* (p. 130)
6. semi
7. hemi
8. demi
9. semi
10. semi

*Fill in the Circle* (p. 131)
11. B          16. C
12. C          17. A
13. D          18. B
14. A          19. B
15. D          20. A

*Which One Doesn't Belong?* (p. 131)
21. retrograde
22. regicide
23. soliloquy
24. microcosm
25. xenocentric

**Unit 32**
*Matching* (p. 132)
1. F      6. B
2. J      7. G
3. H      8. I
4. A      9. C
5. D      10. E

*Numerical Order* (p. 132)
11. G          16. H
12. D          17. E
13. C          18. J
14. B          19. A
15. I          20. F

*Matching* (p. 133)
21. E          26. D
22. F          27. J
23. C          28. G
24. H          29. B
25. I          30. A

*Matching* (p. 133)
31. H          36. A
32. E          37. C
33. F          38. D
34. G          39. J
35. B          40. I

**Unit 29-32 Quiz**
*Matching, Part I* (p. 134)
1. G      6. J
2. B      7. C
3. F      8. E
4. A      9. D
5. H      10. I

*Matching, Part II* (p. 134)
11. D          16. F
12. E          17. G
13. C          18. I
14. H          19. A
15. J          20. B

*Matching, Part III* (p. 135)
21. H
22. I
23. B
24. C
25. E
26. J
27. A
28. G
29. D
30. F

*Matching, Part IV* (p. 135)
31. F
32. E
33. J
34. C
35. I
36. H
37. A
38. G
39. B
40. D